WAR TORN

Caught in Hitler's Germany

❧

P E T E R   H I L G E R

Barringer Publishing, Naples, Florida
www.barringerpublishing.com
Cover, graphics, layout design by Lisa Camp
Editing by Carole Greene

ISBN: 978-0-9891694-4-8

Library of Congress Cataloging-in-Publication Data
War Torn / Peter Hilger

Printed in U.S.A.

The events in this book are actual happenings and people and
their names are real. The author has attempted to describe events
and people as best as he remembers them. But he also wishes
to emphasize that all contents and persons in this book be
treated with respect to the rights of individual privacy.

ACKNOWLEDGEMENTS

❧

I extend my sincerest gratitude to the
Island Writers Group of Sanibel, Florida,
for their outstanding support and encouragement
to write this documentary.

UMKIRCH CASTLE (FRONT) FALL 1944

FRITZ AND PETER, 2009, LAST VISIT TO SIGMARINGEN

CONTENTS

༄

PREFACE

This story is not fiction. I have lived through it all. And thanks to my sheer luck, I came out alive. Some detailed experiences may be rough on your stomach, but they tell what really happened. Some other detailed events you might enjoy and chuckle over.

Originally, my plan was to write this memoir for my family only. As I read it, chapter by chapter, to my writers group, they urged me to share it with a wider audience. I explained to them a solemn promise I had made to my friend Fritz, who figures prominently in several stories in this book. His family name is Hohenzollern. Had Germany still been a monarchy, Fritz would have occupied the throne. He asked me not to publish this book until after his death. He died in September 2010, releasing me from my vow to a friend who was close to me for over sixty-seven years.

Fritz and I maintained contact over all the years since we first met in 1943. One year later he and his generous family hid me from the Gestapo. Had I been discovered as an American civilian in a country at war with America, I knew my fate would be quick and brutal. The Hohenzollerns protected me and, no doubt, saved my life. As I wrote my recollections, I sent him the stories of the time we shared at his estate. He always recalled more details and urged me to include them.

The villain in this story is a brutal dictator who started out to do good things while already thinking of war, conquest and greatness. His name was Adolf Hitler. He influenced my life in more than one way. Most of what I know about him happened during my childhood. Most of what he did to influence my life happened in my early adolescence.

This story is also about what it took for the world to get rid of him. Millions of people on both sides lost their lives while battling him to the end. Many more millions were killed by him in his infamous concentration and death camps. Not all were Jews. His political enemies in the countries he conquered were gassed there as well. Even a Lutheran pastor died in Buchenwald. The minister's life and death were documented in the 2000 PBS movie "Agent of Grace." His name was Bonhöffer, and he was my wife Hanna's uncle.

The first chapter in this book deals with Adolf Hitler. I never met him. So I have attempted to set the stage for what I have to say by drawing a profile of the man from newspaper accounts, interviews conducted by others, quotations from world leaders, books written about him and on some eyewitnesses who had seen and known him. One of these was the aristocratic mother of my good friend Fritz, who was a highly respected saint to me. She was regularly invited to state dinners at the chancellery in Berlin and was invariably seated next to Hitler. She was not a Nazi and definitely not in love with him, but she intelligently used the connection to him for the best protection of her highly visible family. She was also shocked by the immense power this man possessed over women.

As a matter of fact, I have met many people in Germany during these years who were strong—almost fanatic—believers in the dictator. More often than not, they were intellectuals: teachers, lawyers, doctors, philosophers, politicians. The surgeon who in 1937 operated three times on my injured right leg told me of his conviction to say a prayer imploring Hitler to guide him before he went to work on my knee joint and thigh. Without a doubt, I did not make that ritual my habit, but it left a deep impression on me to realize that intelligent people could be so devoted to leaders who are so obviously evil.

After the war, when things normalized and *Der Führer* was gone, many of my American and Canadian friends often asked me: "Why did you not revolt, protest, make noises, 'go on strike' against this man?"

That's easily asked by people living in a free country. If I had opened my mouth to speak just one of those words, my fate would have been certain death in a gas chamber.

I was too young to meet *Der Führer*. Had I been older, I might have gotten to know him, not by choice but by circumstances. With my red hair, freckles and height, I could easily have qualified and been eligible for enlistment into a group of elite *Germanen*—young, blond or red-haired, blue eyed, tall, handsome men—whom Hitler looked for and found to serve in what he termed *Lebensbornheime*—"life-giving homes," in English. Because he was obsessed with the thought to continue the glorious Aryan race forever, he created these establishments all over the country to enable women to be inseminated in dark rooms by those *Germanen* types so that they would give birth to handsome blond, fair, blue-eyed children.

But my wife Hanna did meet him in1937. That day she was turning four. She was one of ten children. Hitler was devoted to families with lots of kids. To him, the children of "the right people," born to families who fit the Aryan picture to a tee, were the ones he worshipped and spoiled. Whenever a child of those large families had a birthday, he or she would be invited to Berlin, to the chancellery, where Hitler would be present to shake their hands. Then they were served chocolate cake. I still have a photo of that event.

But Hanna never realized that he bent down, stretched out his hand and shook hers.

She remembered only the chocolate cake.

ADOLF HITLER, 1889–1945
A PROFILE

ᵔᵔᵔ

This is the story of a dictator's rise and fall from power. As I mentioned in the preface, I was much too young to know from experience how he arrived there. I began to understand this man only at a time when he was already firmly established in his powerful, Caesar-like role of ruling Germany and Europe. So I had to piece together the following biography from newspaper clippings, biographies of others living in his time period, eyewitnesses, hearsay and sections from his book *Mein Kampf*.

He saw the light of this world on the main street of Braunau-am-Inn, a small Austrian border town facing Bavaria across the river. There still stands a modest dwelling currently labeled *"Gasthaus Josef Pommers."* There, on April 20, 1889, was born Alois Schicklgruber, aka Adolf Hitler.

Forty-five years later, Hermann Göring was to say: "We love Adolf Hitler because we believe deeply and unswervingly that God has sent him to us to save Germany." And, again, Hermann Göring after the Blood Purge of June 1934: *"Der Führer* accomplishes great deeds out of the greatness of his heart, the passion of his will and the goodness of his soul. We are all the creatures of *Der Führer.* His faith makes us the most powerful of men. If he removes his confidence, we are nothing. We are plunged into darkness and lost to the memory of man. For Germany is Adolf Hitler." And later Hans Franck, with the fervent benediction of his countrymen: "Hitler is lonely. So is God. Hitler is like God."

"My work," declared Hitler in September 1942, "is the destiny of the *Reich.*"

I was nineteen then and fully realized the madness of this man.

The ultimate judgment of mankind on this man and his work is probably better reflected in the judgment of others. Joseph Stalin, speaking on the 25th anniversary of the Russian Revolution, described Hitler as "a cannibal." Neville Chamberlain said on the day of his resignation as prime minister of Great Britain: "In all history, no other man has been responsible for such a hideous total of human suffering and misery as he."

Hitler's boyhood in Braunau, where his father was a petty *Beamter* (civil servant), was not a happy one. His father bitterly opposed his son's ambition to become an artist. The son came to hate his father but seemingly failed to find solace in love for his mother. It may indeed be doubtful whether at any time in his entire life he ever loved, or was loved by, any normal man or woman.

Still in his teens, he made his way to Vienna where he hoped to study art. After failing his entrance examination into the art academy, he was advised to study architecture. But this was also impossible because he had not graduated from high school. Poverty compelled him to take a job as a laborer. A sense of degradation gnawed on his soul. He found relief in hatred for labor unions, Marxists and also Jews, because these he identified with all he wanted but could not have: wealth, power and culture. "Gradually," he wrote later in his book *Mein Kampf,* "I began to hate them. I was transformed from a weakly world citizen to a fanatic Anti-Semite." In his endless quest for deference and security, he took to painting postcards and selling pictures. But his profits were a pittance and his lot was as humble as before.

He moved to Munich, where he continued to struggle, with little success, to make a living as a commercial artist. With the arrival of World War I in 1914, he fell on his knees and thanked God, his Providence, that he was privileged to live in "heroic" times and to participate in noble deeds of pan-Germanic, Wagnerian splendor. He enlisted in the Bavarian army, although, curiously enough, he retained his Austrian citizenship until 1932.

His record as a soldier from 1914 to 1918 is obscure. He won an iron cross, but his superiors evidently detected in him few signs of leadership or martial genius. He was wounded in 1916 in the battle of the Somme. At the time of the armistice, he was convalescing in a hospital near Berlin from the effects of a gas attack at Ypres.

I was not yet born.

The defeat and capitulation of the *Reich* and exile of its last *Kaiser* to Holland in 1918 meant the collapse of his universe. By his own account, he wept for the first time since the death of his mother and experienced despair and hatred leading him to his decision to enter politics. He now had a mission: that of "regenerating" his countrymen and "saving" them from the Democrats, Marxists, Jews, Masons and other "November criminals." A return to the insecurities of civil life was unthinkable. He remained with his regiment in Munich and became a petty spy and propagandist for reactionary officers.

On a June evening in 1919, Hitler attended a meeting of a German Worker's party where one Gottfried Feder impressed him by demanding the "breaking of the bonds of interest slavery" and distinguishing between "international, Jewish capitalism" and "patriotic, German capitalism" and between "Judeo-Marxist socialism" and pure "national socialism." He was asked to enlist as a member, hesitated, but finally joined as member No.

7. He wrote in his book: "It was the most fateful decision of my life."

Hitler discovered that he was a speaker. Ever larger crowds came to applaud his hoarse denunciations of Versailles and of the Marxists. In the acclaim of the multitude, he found his soul. Presently he was leader. Here, for the first time, he was escaping from his inner anxieties in the face of a world that denied him love.

He gathered about him a group of freeloaders, political murderers and middle-class riffraff. He changed the name of the group to Socialist German Workers' party (N.S.D.A.P, for its German meaning of *National Sozialistische Deutsche Arbeiter Partei).* He borrowed the Roman salute from Mussolini. He organized an *Ordnertruppe* (Order Troop) of rowdies, which later evolved into the brown-shirted Sturmabteilung (S.A.), with the black-uniformed SS as a further refinement in the technique of political gangsterism. In later years, it became known as the *Waffen SS*, the word meaning "weapons" in English. He devised the swastika flag and worked on banners, posters and rituals. He adopted the slogan "Germany, Awake!" from Dietrich Eckart and took over the weird economics of Gottfried Feder.

At that time, I still had not been born.

He and his aides, rummaging around in the musty past for devices to bewitch the masses, concocted a *Weltanschauung* "view of the world" out of all the anti-Christian, anti-western and anti-Semitic elements of German romanticism. A party program was adopted on February 24, 1920, consisting of a frantic mix of pan-Germanism, anti-Semitism, anti-capitalism and "The Common Interest Above Self." Money was solicited from industrialists. Violence was used against trade unions and Social Democrats. The *Kleinbuergertum*, "the masses," cheered. Amid the post-war, Versailles-rooted agony of German despair mostly spurned by an ego-deflating loss of the war, the movement kindled a flame that was ultimately to consume all in its path.

The opportunity came in 1923, the year of the Ruhr invasion, to supplant the occupying French Army and regain access to Germany's important coal and steel mill center, its most prominent being the Krupp Empire of weaponry making. It was as well the year of a disastrous inflation in the German economy.

Hitler perceived that he must strike a bargain with gentlemen of influence if he were to hope for power. Not until a decade later did he learn how to hold his partners to the terms of the compact and then use it to destroy them. His first adventure in the arts of intrigue and revolution culminated in a tragic farce: the "beer hall putsch" and March on Munich's Feldherrenhalle of November 8-9, 1923. Young men died because of his folly. He threatened suicide but changed his mind. He found himself sentenced for treason to the prison fortress of Landsberg-am-Lech, where, at the suggestion of Rudolf Hess, he began writing *Mein Kampf,* "My Fight." It would later become the leading document for the 3rd 1000-year Reich and Adolf Hitler's legacy to his newly acquired fatherland. The republican authorities, always lenient with reactionary plotters, pardoned and released him in December 1924. The "movement" was bankrupt, despite Hitler's industrious efforts to make it a nation-wide party.

The year he went to prison was the year I was born.

The runaway inflation was halted with the introduction of a new *Reichsmark.* For the next five years, most Germans enjoyed the relative prosperity afforded by Anglo-American loans and a high level of business activity. Traditionally, the contented and the hopeful have no use for radical fanaticism. Hitler"s N.S.D.A.P. made no headway.

The world-wide economic depression that began in 1929 created in the stricken Reich a vast new market for political frenzy. Between 1930 and 1932 the N.S.D.A.P. became the largest party in Germany, thanks to mass unemployment and bourgeois desperation. Hitler almost got himself elected to the presidency of the Republic in opposition to Paul von Hindenburg, to whose support all conservative democrats and liberals rallied as a means of thwarting the *Nazis,* as Hitler's followers became known. As the business cycle swung slightly upward in the fall of 1932, the Nazi votes again declined and Goebbels wrote in his diary in December: "For hours on end, the Führer walks up and down in his hotel room. Once he stops and says: `If the Party should ever break up, I'll make an end of things in three minutes with a revolver.'"

I was nine years old.

But then occurred what had happened many times before and what was to take place over and over again in the future: the rescue of the destroyers by those who were to be destroyed. Thanks to the conspiracy of January 1933, concocted by leading German industrialists, politicians and organizations, Franz Von Papen, Baron Von Schroeder, Fritz Thyssen, Alfred Hugenberg, the *Reichsverband der Industrie* ("Federation of Industry") and the *Junker Landbund* (a loosely organized group of the mostly aristocratic, young and upcoming), and last, but not least, Hindenburg.

Shortly after the Russian Revolution broke out in 1917, General Ludendorf, second in command at that time, without the knowledge of Hindenburg, arranged for the passage through Germany of Lenin, the Bolshevist agitator then living in Switzerland but anxious to return to Russia. Lenin reached Petrograd (which was later renamed Leningrad until the Soviet Union broke up in the 1990s, when it again became St. Petersburg) and at once launched a campaign for peace. The morale of the Russian armies was seriously affected. Although Alexander Kerensky, the minister of war, was able to restore it sufficiently for an offensive in July 1917, its fighting spirit was definitely broken. When the Bolshevists came to power in November of that year, they promptly proposed an armistice, and the Central Powers accepted.

WAR TORN

Ever since that happening, the aged Field Marshall was either retired or called back to duty. He played various roles in the tumultuous *Weimar Republik* between 1919 and 1933. During the previous year, Franz Von Papen, a close friend but a deep intriguer, was succeeded by General Von Schleicher, another favorite, only to be ousted in January 1933. Adolf Hitler's National Socialists were now the strongest party in Germany, and Hitler had made a bid for power in the summer of 1932.

Hindenburg refused to appoint "that Bohemian corporal," but in January 1933 he was persuaded to do so by Von Papen, who thought that he and the other experienced politicians of the right could manipulate the upstart Viennese paperhanger. It should be mentioned here that the old marshal had become somewhat senile. In all probability, he did not understand the machinations of those around him, including his son Oskar, who had allowed the estate of Neudeck, East Prussia—donated to Hindenburg by admiring Junkers, so named because they were young, revolutionary aristocrats from large landowner families—to be registered in his own name in order to escape the payment of inheritance tax in case his father should die.

The calculations of Papen were quickly and completely frustrated by Hitler, who was soon able to propel himself to complete power.

Hindenburg's career was now practically ended, although Hitler treated him with marked respect, and the distinguished old general spent increasingly more time at Neudeck. When Hitler carried through his purge on June 30, 1934, a telegram was sent from Neudeck congratulating him on having "nipped treason in the bud and saved the German nation from serious danger." It bore Hindenburg's signature; whether it was actually signed by him remains uncertain. On August 2, 1934, he died at his family home in Neudeck,

So the conspiracy of 1933 used the aged Hindenburg as their willing tool, and the son of Alois Schicklgruber found himself chancellor of the

15

Reich on January 30, 1933.

The tale of how he and his aides destroyed the German Republic by treachery and deceit, built a totalitarian tyranny upon foundations of intolerance and terrorism, re-armed the Reich and ultimately enslaved Europe is the tale of what Konrad Heiden, perhaps Hitler's most acute biographer, once called *das Zeitalter der Verantwortungslosigkeit* – "the epoch of irresponsibility." Hitler became Caesar over Europe because of the prodigious power of self-deception that some influential Europeans, Britons and Americans displayed in the face of a menace they failed to understand and in some cases even mistook for salvation. The most notable of them was no other than Charles Lindbergh. The man who fled from reality into fantasy and became a devil thereby was able to turn his fantasies into realities because his victims everywhere were blinded by their own insecurities to the old and simple distinctions between what is actual and what is illusion, what is true and what is false, what is good and what is evil.

Thus, Adolf Hitler declared January 30, 1933, the beginning of the 1,000-year *3rd Reich*.

I was nine years old.

That infamous day in Germany's history, Hitler set out to soften the mood of her population. He came to power in a political vacuum. During the preceding fourteen years, the *Weimar Republik* had brought a devastating inflation to the country. It changed prime ministers regularly, sometimes every other month. It culminated in the Great Depression. Germany was ripe for change.

All went well at first. Poverty was more or less eliminated, beggars disappeared, the economy was cranked up, the streets were clean, the houses freshly painted and the Volkswagen was born, meaning *"people's car"* in German. A car for everybody! The price was uniformly—meaning no frills—set at Reichsmark 1,000.00, or $238.00 in the currency of the time.

A huge new factory using Ford's system of assembly lines was built in Wolfsburg, west of Berlin, where the *Kaefer*, "beetle," in English, as they were later actually called—was cranked out by the thousands. Hitler's other motif—which he did not tell the German people—was to have a facility ready to build tanks and Jeep-type vehicles for the military actions he had already envisioned. To this day, the plant still builds Volkswagens, but no longer the beetle.

The first *Autobahn* appeared between Frankfurt and Heidelberg. The economy was roaring. When more money was needed, Hitler had it printed or minted—never mind gold-backed currency or GNP-based. Life was good. Or so it seemed.

I was still only thirteen years old in 1937, when clouds began to appear on Germany's horizon. It was the year when, in May, disaster happened in Lakehurst, NJ. On the 6th of that month, the Flagship of the German Zeppelins, the LZ 129, named after the well-known German General and former President Paul von Hindenburg, burned while attempting to land at the U.S. Naval Base. The airship was filled with seven million cubic feet of hydrogen capable of lifting 247,000 pounds. The gas was highly flammable and used in lieu of the non-flammable helium not available for Germany in those days. Its maximum speed was eighty-seven miles per hour as powered by four Daimler Benz diesel engines. It was three times as long as a Boeing 747 introduced in 1961.

The airship had encountered strong headwinds along the East Coast of the United States and was over twelve hours late.

Experts think that the sudden turning-into-the-wind landing maneuver of the dirigible had caused the combustion. U.S. Navy Chief Petty Officer R.H.Ward observed the landing from the top of the mooring mast: "Captain Max Pruss may have been in a hurry to bring the ship to the ground due to the intense thunderstorm activity which resulted in a lot of electrical static in the air. He made a rather tight turn during its final approach. Gas was vented to bring the ship into trim. During the last eleven minutes of the flight, the ship was tail heavy, so 2,000 lbs of water was dropped from the stern."

The gas apparently leaked out of its rear gas bag and combined with air. Thus, it became a highly combustible mixture that at once started to burn wildly and bring down the airship in only thirty-four seconds.

Thirty-six people died.

At that time, the Hindenburg had completed its sixty-third flight and had logged over 3,000 hours of reliable service. All German Zeppelins still in use at the time of the collapse were grounded indefinitely. They never flew again.

The tragic news was, of course, broadcast every half hour on the German State Radio, which played a portion of the death song from *Brahms' Requiem* before and after. Propaganda was, for a change, left out of the newscast. I heard it all on my *Volksempfaenger* radio shortly after it happened. I heard it many times over and over again during the subsequent days. Malcolm at the BBC rendered a less somber version of the accident but nevertheless one that was full of sorrow for the loss of the airship and its passengers and crew.

The Hindenburg was Germany's pride and joy. Hitler used it to demonstrate the achievement of the supreme Aryan race over non-existing transportation devices anywhere else in the world. For Germany and its regime, it was a huge loss of pride and prestige.

But political clouds as well began to appear in 1937. Hitler instigated and executed his campaign to eliminate the Jews by destroying their possessions, throwing them out the windows into the streets during one long night. It was an action uniformly executed throughout Germany's larger cities and became known as *Kristallnacht*, "crystal night."

I was only thirteen years old.

Shortly thereafter, the first concentration camps sprang up in Germany.

That drastic fact was never, ever broadcast to the German populace. If people close to the regime or otherwise had heard of them, circumstances forced them to be silent. The nature of a dictatorship does not provide room for lack of discretion. If my dad, who undoubtedly knew about the facility's existence, would have ever dared to tell us kids about it, and we would have proudly pronounced out loud our knowledge to our friends in school, we could have instantly ended up in those camps as well. After the war ended, many people asked me if I knew. I gave them all the above answer.

Later still during that tumultuous year 1937, Hitler occupied the *Sudetenland*, a portion of Czechoslovakia surrounding the country on three sides like a ring. Historically, it had primarily been settled by Germans. He claimed it for the fatherland.

In 1938 he annexed his native Austria and "brought it back home to the fatherland as well." The dark clouds on the political horizon began to be severe and threatening.

The western European countries, England and France, were rightfully alarmed. British Prime Minister Chamberlain and his French counterpart Daladier went to Germany twice, once to Bad Godesberg and once to Munich, to meet with *Der Führer* to convince him to end the *Landschluckerei*, the annexation of land belonging to other nations. From each of these meetings, the British and French leaders returned to their respective capitals to report that Hitler was highly responsive to their requests and made all sorts of promises to stop the aggression.

It was a perfect case of appeasement; historians now recognize that Hitler never intended to end his expansion. He had declared Germany to be a country *ohne Grenzen* – "without borders."

During the spring of 1939, he marched into Czechoslovakia. During the early summer of 1939, he sent his foreign minister von Ribbentrop to Moscow to negotiate a Non-Aggression Pact with the Soviet Union.

19

At that time, my uncle Gustav Hilger, a member of our "Russian" part of the family, was *Botschaftsrat* of the German Embassy in Moscow. In numerous newspapers of that period, he was seen sitting between Stalin and von Ribbentrop, undoubtedly translating for both. He had been born in Russia and spoke the language without as much as a tiny flaw.

It was all a pre-calculated move to keep the Soviet Union quiet while he occupied other countries in Europe. But he probably planned all along that at some future date Russia would also have to be conquered.

A month later, on September 1st, Hitler ordered his Wehrmacht to march into Poland. World War II had begun!

I was all of sixteen years old.

His allies were Generalissimo Franco in Spain and Benito Mussolini in Italy, both severe dictators, as was he. Japan, on the other side of the globe, was his partner as well. Their alliance was called the Axis. They made sure Sweden, Switzerland and Portugal stayed neutral and untouched. Their riches were stashed in Swiss banks, and they needed the safe houses for all of the world's spies in Lisbon and Stockholm for much needed contacts with enemies and exchange of information.

Many people in Germany wept because they expected the much better equipped Allied Forces to overcome the *Fatherland* at once.

Yet what people did not remember—or even know—was what General de Gaulle had already predicted in 1932. After spending some time observing maneuvers of the German Army, he commented in a speech to the *Assemble Nationale* in Paris: "When that Army attacks us, we will be instantly defeated."

He was right.

France was overrun the following spring. But not only *La Grande Nation* but Poland, Holland, Belgium, Denmark, Norway, Yugoslavia, Albania, Hungary and Greece were all defeated by Hitler's armed forces.

Yet he had not conquered and occupied the land of his foremost enemy:

England. So a secret plan to cross the channel was prepared before Goebbels started his Blitz propaganda machine to shout in speeches and on the radio his message that Great Britain must no longer be great but must be brought to her knees by the victorious German Armed Forces. The slogan in public was accompanied by a song the SA, HJ, BDM, and SS were forced to sing in public:

Denn wir fahren, denn wir fahren gen Engel-land

('cause we're driving, we're driving towards Angle-land!)

His generals, however, warned that in view of his plans in the east, a trek across the channel and the monumental task to conquer and occupy a land well-equipped to defend itself was not advisable. The military action never materialized. At that time in his reign, *Der Führer* still listened to his military leaders, who were supposed to make his dreams as master of the world a reality.

In early 1941, he declared war on Russia. That turned out to be his first big mistake. Not until that year did the barbarism which Hitler had summoned up out of the tortured depths of the German soul encounter an obstacle it could not corrupt or crush. At the end of that year, having conquered and occupied most of Europe, he boasted of his greatest triumphs when entering the Soviet Union from the west. While rendering one of his three-hour speeches, he hollered at a monstrous rally in the Nuremberg Arena: "God up to now has placed the stamp of approval on our battle. It is the will of the democratic war-inciters, and their Jewish-capitalistic manipulators, that the war must be continued. The year 1941 will bring completion of the greatest victory in our history."

I was, of course, glued to the German State Radio by day whenever I had the time, and the BBC with the familiar voice of Malcolm during the late evening hours, with my radio under my pillow. Goebbels had meanwhile introduced the dramatic effect his *Sondermeldungen*, "special announcements of great urgency," would achieve by each newscast being preceded with the first few notes of Beethoven's fifth symphony, a series of staccato, full-orchestra-intoned thundering bursts of music in dramatic tone, tact and sequence.

Not until 1941, in the heroism of the Red army, did the Nazi fanatics meet a foe capable of inflicting upon them a decisive military defeat. The march to the outskirts of Moscow had still excited the regime. But the Soviets blocked it west of the capital and at Leningrad. The Wehrmacht never went further. The battle stagnated.

A year later, the bloody battles begun in 1942 for Leningrad in the north of Russia and Stalingrad in southern Ukraine became the turning point and caused huge losses of German and Russian lives and war equipment. In early 1943, the Germans began their retreat.

Little known was the fact that my wife's oldest brother, Count Rüdiger von der Goltz—who had fulfilled a long-standing family tradition that the oldest son of an aristocratic family serve in the elite regiment of the country—was killed in the battle for the city the Germans never conquered: Moscow!

❖

Early in 1942, his remains were sent to the family's farm: Kinsegg, in Bavaria. Subsequently they buried him alongside some of his ancestors under an ancient oak tree on a hill belonging to the land. But I and a great number of others started to wonder why his body arrived for burial. Those killed in action were traditionally buried in mass graves at the spot where they were killed. Why was an exception made for Rüdiger? Was it because he was a Count? Surely not, and unlikely under Hitler's reign. Rumors appeared in the 1980s that he was rather killed by Himmler's Waffen SS for muttering severe criticism of the regime and its warfare.

❖

Then in December 1941, after the Japanese attack on Pearl Harbor, the self-proclaimed leader assured the German people by saying: "The assault was well deserved. But do not worry. Because although the Americans can produce excellent razor blades, they are lousy soldiers."

I don't remember where I was or what I thought at that moment. What I do remember is that the German radio stations announced this major event scantily then fell silent. Historians told me later that Germany had hoped Japan would declare war on Russia. That didn't happen. But Japan was allied with Germany and Italy through Axis. That made Hitler declare war on the United States two weeks later.

And that turned out to be his second major mistake.

I was eighteen years old. And overnight I had become a foreign national in an enemy country.

❖

Both of these declarations of war—on the Soviet Union and the United States of America—ended with the total collapse of his 1,000-year 3rd Reich on May 8, 1945. But consider the lives it cost both sides to eliminate the dictatorship and the man embracing it! Their losses reached into the millions.

❖

Meanwhile, the corporal from Braunau matured without mellowing and remained, for all his "greatness," a twisted caricature of the little man, driven to fury by overcompensations for his own inadequacies. In the international crises preceding World War II, he found that it was still politically advantageous to indulge in maniacal ravings. But the actual state of his emotional and mental life remained a mystery to the outside world.

Hitler lived simply amid the luxury of the chancellery, the *Führerhaus* and the "Eagle's Nest" above Berchtesgaden, the extravagant villa he ordered to be built on top of a lone rock above the town where he ultimately celebrated so many of his triumphs. In his entourage, he had fanatical worshippers galore. But no man or woman was bound to him by reciprocal affection. He read cheap novels for recreation and put on weight by virtue of good food and a slowly growing lethargy. For

Germans still dream-driven, he remained a Messiah. To the outer world, he seemed more and more a demon.

Of the *Führer* on the eve of war, Sir Neville Henderson, Britain's last ambassador to the Third *Reich*, wrote: "He was, he said, fifty years old; he preferred war now rather than when he would be fifty-five or sixty. Though he spoke of his artistic tastes and of his longing to satisfy them, I derived the impression that the corporal of the last war was even more anxious to prove what he could do as the conquering generalissimo of the next."

On September 1, 1939, Hitler told the *Reichstag*: "I desire nothing other than to be the first soldier of the German *Reich*. I have again put on that old coat which was the most sacred and the most dear to me of all. I will not take it off until the victory is ours or I shall not live to see the end. There is one word that I have never learned: capitulation."

Of the Führer of 1942, U.S. Vice-President Henry A. Wallace said: "The belief in one Satan-inspired leader is the last and ultimate darkness. In a twisted sense, there is something almost great in the figure of the supreme devil operating through a human form, in a Hitler who has the daring to spit straight into the eye of God and man. But the Nazi system has a heroic position for only one leader. All the rest are stooges and psychopathic cases. Satan has turned loose upon us the insane."

He had conquered most of Europe. But having failed to conquer Britain, Hitler attacked Russia. Having failed to conquer Russia, Hitler and his Asiatic allies attacked America. "A historic revenge has been entrusted to us by the Creator," he declared on December 11, 1941. "I consider Roosevelt to be insane. We know, of course, that the eternal Jew is behind all this. Our patience has come to the breaking point."

❖

These steps situated him definitely in the ranks of those whom the Gods would destroy. The birth and growth of the United Nations placed the seal of ultimate doom upon the career of the mad Reichskanzler and his people.

❖

The close of this tortured career was an episode in the global holocaust perpetrated by the forces that had made Hitler their tool and mouthpiece. Defeat before Moscow in the fall of 1941 foreshadowed the turning point of World War II at El Alamein in Africa and Stalingrad in Russia sixteen months later. The year 1943 saw the Führer's vision of world hegemony slowly fade in the consuming fires of Allied counterattack. During 1944, the Wehrmacht was driven from Rome (June 4), Minsk (July 3), Paris (August 25), Bucharest (August 31) Sofia (September 16), Belgrade and Athens (October 1).

That summer of 1944, Rudolf Hess, Hitler's designated assistant and successor, had a *Luftwaffe* pilot fly him to England, to enable him to talk to Chamberlain and arrange an armistice. Hitler was not informed of this plan. Hess's desertion was seen by him as treason on the fatherland. He raged in the chancellery in Berlin and made Göbbels announce the developments on the radio.

The military disaster of retreat moved a group of army leaders to attempt to save Germany from complete catastrophe. On July 20, 1944, the Berlin radio cancelled an announced program on "The Extermination of Rats" to declare that Hitler had been the victim of assassins.

Col. Count Claus von Stauffenberg had left a time bomb in a briefcase at Hitler's headquarters. *Der Führer* was bruised and burned by the explosion. The plot was widespread. Its organizers included Field Marshal Erwin Von Witzleben, Generals Friedrich Olbricht, Erich Hoepner, Kurt Zeitzler and Ludwig Beck, Admiral Wilhelm Canaris, Dr. Karl Gördeler, Baron Ullrich Von Hassel, Count Wolf Von Helldorf, and thousands more, all of whom were, without trial, instantly shot or hanged or took their own lives.

I had just turned twenty-one six weeks before. I was old enough to understand the political process, to comprehend the magnitude of his destructive policy on Germany, to become shocked over the loss of so many lives in the attempt to destroy one evil emperor, to deploy more intense and concentrated air raids and thus the progressing destruction of the country that increased in intensity in an Allied effort to bring the war to a close.

And I had so intensely wished *Der Führer* could be wiped out forever.

Graf Rüdiger von der Goltz, a brilliant and well-known Berlin attorney, who would become my father-in-law eight years later, was also involved in the July 1944 assassination attempt but did not get caught. This was even more astonishing for the fact that shortly before, he had defended one of Hitler's generals in a celebrated trial that accused the general of being a homosexual. Rüdiger had him acquitted of all charges but undoubtedly remained on Hitler's black list. And the acquitted general died shortly thereafter by way of a "tragic car accident," or so the propaganda machine said. Himmler's *Waffen SS* had been at work again.

❖

Irony had it that Count Rüdiger, who had escaped the Russians in Berlin moments before they took the city, was taken into custody by the American Military Government in Heidelberg when he arrived at his ranch in Bavaria. He spent a year in a light-security safe house near Frankfurt and was ultimately acquitted of all charges, de-nazified, as they termed it in those days. He went to Düsseldorf and started a new law practice from scratch, which was taken over by his son and is now in the hands of his grandson, with some eighty attorneys in three European cities.

❖

As a result, the failure of the conspiracy meant that the nation was doomed to share the *Götterdämmerung* of its demented ruler.

In November 1944, Hitler proclaimed that "Sovietism, supported by the democracies, is endeavoring to destroy the Reich and exterminate our people. The Jew is the destroying manipulator of democracy as he is the creator and inciter of the Bolshevik world-beast."

In his last New Year's Day speech, Hitler still promised victory. In his last, twelfth anniversary, speech on January 30, 1945, he shouted old clichés and called for "every sacrifice" and the "utmost fanaticism." "I shall be happy," he declared on February 24, "to bear all that the others have to bear. The only thing that I should not be able to bear would be the weakness of my nation. The life that is left to us should serve only one task: namely to make up for all the wrongs done by the international Jewish criminals and their henchmen to our nation. Twenty-five years ago I predicted the victory of our movement. Today I predict the final victory of the German race."

On April 20, 1945, his fifty-sixth birthday, Hitler was silent.

On May 1, 1945, as Berlin's death agony approached its final stage and the 3rd Army led by Patton prepared to enter Braunau-am-Inn, Admiral Karl Doenitz proclaimed himself *Führer* and announced that Hitler had fallen at his post in the chancellery. "Faithful to his great ideal of saving the nations of Europe from Bolshevism, he has given his life and has met a hero's death."

Eight days later, on May 8, 1945, his 1,000-year 3rd Reich collapsed, by General Jodl's signature, in Berlin, via a document that specified total and unconditional surrender.

Consider the lives it cost both sides to eliminate the dictatorship and the man incorporating it! It reached into the millions.

I was twenty-two years old.

The government of Portugal proclaimed two days' mourning. Officials in Madrid and Tokyo were saddened. Eamon de Valera extended condolences to the German Embassy in Dublin.

The rest of the world rejoiced.

HILGER FOREBEARS

Seeing the title of this documentary, you might ask: "Why was he, the author, an American civilian in Germany while both nations were at war with each other?" So allow me to explain. I will start out by telling you a bit about my family history.

I was born in Germany to an American father and a Dutch mother. According to U.S. law, that made me an American citizen. According to German law, it made me an alien that consisted of fifty percent Dutch, twenty-five percent English and twenty-five percent German origins.

Let me start with the easiest, the Dutch part: My mother was one-hundred percent Dutch. We trace her family back to the early 1600s. My father's mother contributed the English in me; the German came from my father's father Hilger. We know the first time that name was mentioned in our records was in 1594, with the name Peter Heiliger, meaning "Saint." The surname later changed to Hilliger then to Hilger, as it remains today.

I am somewhat dazzled by the more recent family history because looking at our Hilger *Stammbaum*, German for "family tree," I find families with lots of children. Since Peter Heiliger, all of them were born and lived their lives in Remscheid, Germany, a mill town in the hills east of Cologne. Take my great-grandfather, for instance. His name was Gustav Hilger, and he lived from 1814 to 1897, at that time a long, rewarding life of 83 years. When he was eighteen, his father retained him at home to enter and ultimately lead the family enterprise *Gebrüder Hilger*. Or, in English, "Hilger Brothers." They were manufacturers of a variety of tools: knives, forks, spoons and other eating utensils needed in the fatherland in those days. Gustav may have exported to neighboring European countries, but I cannot find details of such activity and must therefore only assume he did.

But what impressed me much more is the number of children he had with his wife Marie Johanna Alexandrine, whose maiden name was Hasenclever, and the sequences of their birth and the span of their lives. Here is the list:

Ernst	1844 to 1900
Walter	1846 to 1905
Helene	1847 to 1924
Clara	1848 to 1937
Peter Caspar	**1849 to 1930**
Robert	1851 to 1851
Gustav	1852 to 1936
Marie	1854 to 1932
Johanna	1855 to 1916
Otto	1857 to 1945
Elizabeth	1859 to 1938
Hugo	1861 to 1862

Five daughters and seven sons in seventeen years! Of these twelve children, two—Robert and Hugo—died as infants, but ten lived on through considerably long lives.

The one in bold letters is my grandfather. One son in every generation since 1594 was named Peter, at first, then Peter Caspar from the 1700s onward. Actually, according to family tradition, it was up to my father's youngest brother, Peter Caspar, to pass on the name. But when it became evident that he would not marry anyone, my grandparents prevailed on my father to continue the tradition. Soon thereafter I came along. But my mom had trouble with the name and wanted me to be named Gerhard first. Voila! I became Gerhard Peter Caspar. But I wanted to be Peter. I passed the name on to one of my sons. We named him Axel Peter Caspar, and he named his son Ryan Peter Caspar. It may all be a bit confusing to you, I guess, but not to my family.

Gustav, the father of them all, had a very practical idea when his kids grew up. He trained his oldest son to remain in Remscheid to be his successor in the firm. He picked four of his other sons to go abroad and be the direct factory representative in their destination countries. Ernst stayed at home; my grandfather came to New York; Walter went to Tientsin, China; Gustav was sent to Moscow, Russia; Otto went to Sidney, Australia. Then he ran out of sons, so instead he picked Hugo Friederichs, the husband of his daughter Johanna, to go to Rio de Janeiro.

Gustav, now in Moscow, married a Russian lady, and all his children were born in Moscow. Walter married an English lady and his kids were all born in China. Otto married in Sidney, but I have no record of whom he wed. The Friederichs had a number of Brazilian offspring. And finally my grandfather married Bertha Harriett. More of that will follow below.

Walter's children and children's children fled China shortly after the Chinese Revolution in 1949. They went to Hamburg to live, but not surprisingly, left Germany again a year later. The country really did not mean anything to them. They settled in Bangkok, where they remain to this day.

The entire Friederichs clan still lives in Brazil and Argentina.

❖

At a glamorous, super-upscale party in a penthouse of downtown Buenos Aires in 2001, a very good-looking woman—in her mid forties, I guessed, but looking more like early thirties—approached me in the crowd of over 100 guests and asked: "Permisso, but are you Pedro?"

"Yes, I am. But how do you know my name?"

"Rosemarie, our hostess, told me your name and that you are from the United States. And your last name is Hilger, right?"

"Correct on both counts," I replied while studying the deeply-cut front of her very tight-fitting dress, her shapely legs and the tallest high heels I had ever seen.

"Then we are cousins!"

"Cousins? I have no cousins here. Aside from our host and hostess, I don't know anyone here in Argentina."

"Now you know me. I live here with my husband, but I was born in Rio de Janeiro."

"But how am I your cousin?"

"My grandmother, Johanna Hilger, was a sister of your grandfather Peter Caspar. She emigrated to Brazil with my grandfather Friederich, a few years after your grandfather arrived in New York. So we are cousins twice removed, I guess." Then she gently touched my arm and said: "Here, come with me. I want you to meet my husband. He is into railroads."

"Okay," I said, following her leading arm near my elbow, giving me slight but noticeable squeezes of recognition with her slender hand.

Her hubby turned out to be the one and only guest wearing a tie and jacket in this scorching summer heat of a December day in Argentina. I was not surprised when I heard he was a Brit. My cousin excitedly introduced me. "Enchanted," he said, then turned to talk to other guests.

❖

My family scattered around the world to live in "retirement" in Rome, Lugano and Paris. When they came back to the U.S. for their obligatory annual visit and we had them over for dinner, I would ask them: "Why don't you spend more time here in your home country?"

"Oh well, we don't like all your food being deep-freezed. Over in Europe they don't do that. Our servants go to the market every day to buy it fresh. But we can see that you do that as well, Hanna, don't you? It is so much more delicious. Like your steaks tonight."

Okay, surely another point of view. But none of them would ever know that the steaks they ate at our house had been in the deep freeze for months.

I am the only one of our extended family who returned to this country to live.

In 1952, the Hilger clan had its last family reunion at an old castle near Remscheid, Germany. Hilger family members assembled, numbering 158 and speaking five different languages: German, Russian, Spanish, Chinese and Portuguese. I met numerous cousins who did not understand me, and vice versa.

We have not had a reunion since.

All of Gustav senior's emissaries to other countries succeeded well in their businesses of representing the mother company in Remscheid. All of them contributed substantially to her growth into a steel mill with over 3,000 employees. Its name was changed from *Gebrüder Hilger* to BSI, standing for *Bergische Stahlindustrie*. In the 1970s, shareholders—still only family members—numbered in the hundreds. Everybody wanted to live well on dividends but nobody was willing to re-invest in the company. So for lack of family-generated capital, the BSI was offered to Thyssen Steel, Germany's second largest steel mill, and later was sold to them in return for shares in Thyssen.

His son Gustav's Russian clan, all Russian-born but claimed by the Bolsheviks to be of German origin, were shipped to imprisonment in Siberia in 1917, then sent back to Germany in 1919. Most of them settled in Remscheid again.

But Gustav junior, grandson of the family patriarch Gustav with twelve children, did not stay in Remscheid long. A year later, in 1920, the then first German government after WWI, known in history books as the *Weimar Republik,* wanted to re-open a mission rather than an embassy in Russia. When Gustav heard about it, he immediately applied and was instantly hired to be the mission's first chief, although he was a born Russian citizen.

Over the years, the German Foreign Office never named him ambassador, not because he was unqualified but because that would have meant a change in that post by every government, depending on which party was in charge, as such positions are normally filled by political appointments. So *Botschaftsrat,* the highest civil service rank a professional government civil servant could reach, was the title Gustav carried until 1941, when Hitler marched into Russia.

His photograph was on the front page of every European newspaper in mid-August 1939, when he sat between Stalin and the German foreign minister, Von Ribbentrop, to translate for both what was to be agreed upon, namely the non-aggression pact Hitler wanted from Russia. *Der Führer's* motif was quite clear: he wanted Russia to be at ease about his intentions to march into Poland first, then into France half a year later. He did this to link East Prussia again with Germany and, in the process, take Danzig as well, the only Baltic Sea port city Poland had. He thus created more *Lebensraum* for his countrymen, the slogan Hitler regularly used to expand his occupied space around all of Europe.

Russia demanded—and received—guarantees that they in turn could march into Poland from the East to claim their part in the deal. So Poland was to be divided between the two countries.

On September 1, 1939, a week after the pact was signed by von Ribbentrop and Molotov, the Soviet foreign minister, in the presence of Stalin and with Gustav looking on, Hitler's Wehrmacht entered Poland.

World War II had begun.

But when Hitler had conquered most of Europe two years later, he sent his Wehrmacht to attack Russia by crossing the line through Poland that separated the two countries. Stalin considered that fact a severe breach of the non-aggression pact he had signed with the Hitler regime in the presence of Gustav.

So, in violation of all internationally accepted diplomatic rules, he ordered his underlings to load the entire staff of the German Embassy into railroad freight cars, with some food and water thrown in as well. Then the doors were shut and locked. Eight weeks later, they were opened again—in Turkey.

Gustav and his Russian wife (Marie) Mary, both born Russian citizens still, spent the war years living in Berlin and working for Hitler's Foreign Ministry. At war's end they fled to Frankfurt before the Soviets conquered Berlin. But the Soviets immediately kidnapped a well-known German physicist, Professor Heiseman at the university in Kassel, located in the British occupation zone, and whisked him to Russia. Considering Gustav a prime target as a witness of Russian Bolshevism at work, Washington feared similar acts by the Soviets to follow.

Therefore, two days after VE-Day, the State Department asked the American Army for an immediate rescue mission. The Pentagon responded at once. An American Army captain, accompanied by his assisting lieutenant and twenty-some beefy GIs with empty trucks, knocked on Gustav's and Mary's door at two in the morning and informed them that they needed to pack an overnight bag at once.

"We take you along to nearby Rhein Main Air Force Base," said the captain in accented German. "Do not fear us. We will fly you on a military plane immediately and, without one more moment of hesitation, to Washington, where you will be out of reach of the Russians. The plane is stocked with food, filled up with fuel and ready to take off the minute we get there."

Aunt Mary told me much later in Washington that at first they were aghast and frightened, because they thought that now the Americans would take them prisoners. "I was beside myself and scared beyond belief when I heard the knock. It sounded so much like what the Bolsheviks would do in our homeland."

But when they arrived at the airport still in the deep, dark night, another Army officer, who was going to escort them all the way to Washington, assured them: "This is just an urgently needed rescue mission for both of you to be out of Russian reach. Settle down and relax. I will have the steward bring you a nice, big American breakfast after we take off."

After proper de-briefing at the undisclosed location of a safe house, Gustav became advisor of Russian Affairs to the U.S. Department of State.

"I was somewhat anxious to leave our few remaining Russian treasures behind. But the captain said that all of our belongings would be loaded on a truck by the group of GIs he had brought along, for shipment by separate plane to the U.S.," Mary said much later in Washington. "I looked at all those huge soldiers, who had such bulky muscles, and I was terrified of how they would handle our precious icons and paintings."

But everything arrived intact and for many years adorned their Washington apartment and their country farmhouse in Western Maryland. It turned out that nothing broke—not even Mary's most fragile, paper-thin teacups. Because she used them to serve my tea at five in the afternoon when, during late fall of 1950, I was briefly stationed in Washington and saw them frequently. On weekends, I would drive them out to their farm in my 1936 Ford and even helped them rake leaves on the seemingly endless grasslands surrounding their farmhouse dating back to the late 1800s.

Aunt Mary would prepare healthy and plentiful Russian dishes for dinner, and we would talk way into the night. Both still had a harsh, guttural accent in their German and, of course, their English as well. They never lost it throughout the rest of their lives. Gustav explained it to me one evening: "Russian is a very guttural language. It is dominated by the sounds originating in your throat. It is the easternmost language of continental Europe. But have you ever noticed that going west, European languages tend to become softer and your tongue moves forward? As in Russian to Polish to German to French to Spanish and ending up in Portuguese, which is spoken with your tongue practically at your front teeth?"

"That's amazing, Uncle. I never thought of that."

"Yes, it is true. But there is another aspect to these phenomena. The human tongue can easily adjust to being moved forward, but has great difficulties moving backwards. For a Portuguese speaker to learn Russian is practically impossible. Even French is difficult for them. But Russians easily learn any language spoken in countries west of them."

"So that's the reason you and Aunt Mary speak German and English so well?"

"Indeed."

In 1952, he and Aunt Mary returned to West Germany. Gustav re-joined the Foreign Ministry in Bonn, now as an ambassador emeritus, which included a few years of teaching at Germany's School for Diplomats in Speyer, 223 kilometers south of the German capital.

In 1953, he finished writing a book about his twenty-one years as head of the German Mission in Moscow, titled *Wir und der Kreml* in German, and in the United States "The Incompatible Ally," a Memoir-History of German-Soviet Relations 1918 - 1941, the latter co-written for correct English by Alfred G. Meyer and published by Alfred Metzner Verlag, Frankfurt, Germany and by The Macmillan Company, New York respectively. Both books sold out in three weeks.

A second book, simply titled *Stalin*, was written and published only in German by Musterschmidt Verlag, Goettingen in 1959.

He and Mary never returned to their beloved Moscow, where both had been born and raised and spent most of their lives. Gustav was pensioned in 1960, and both lived in a retirement home in Munich until his death in 1968. Mary followed him five months later.

So what happened to Peter Caspar, my paternal grandfather? In 1874 his father, the family patriarch Gustav, sent him to the United States on a slow freighter. It took three weeks to cross the big pond. He was then twenty-five years old and had learned all about the paternal business he needed to know for his future role in it. He settled down in New York City. He found an inexpensive warehouse-type apartment that was already occupied and shared by other immigrants. It was located in the Soho section of New York, at the edge of what in those days was the northern end of the city. Then he set up shop in downtown as the new representative of his family's firm in Remscheid.

Four years later, in 1878, he married my grandmother Bertha Harriett Medlicot Fleitman, of English descent. To fulfill a promise made to his stern new father-in-law to provide well for his young bride, he moved out of Soho to the edge of town, the Murray Hill Section in the area between 30th and 32nd streets in what is now midtown. Kids arrived in rapid succession: two daughters, Tillie in 1879 and Lulu in 1880. Through Google in 2006, I found them listed in the 1881 census of New York and specifically Murray Hill, but the four children were not mentioned. Yet they had added two other names "of Irish descent," who turned out to be their two servants.

Two sons followed in 1882 and 1885.

With four children now, the apartment in Murray Hill became crowded. So they built a house "way out in the country" on the corner of

72nd street and Fifth Avenue. The "EL" on Madison had just been extended as a suburban transportation means to 70th street, so commuting to Wall Street was made easy.

Their house was a brownstone. They are still around in all parts of the city. My grandparents lived in one that had a stamp-sized front yard between the front door, reachable by a stone staircase, and the tree-lined sidewalk, but a larger back yard where they kept the products of their devotion: flowers and exotic plants of all sizes and shapes. Their gardener was a mixture of Dutch and German.

The year before, Central Park had been conceived as a grand feature of the future New York, and the press decried the city council for squandering the precious means of support for so many New Yorkers on a folly like a few pieces of rock and scrubby growth as a future "park" for the growing city.

❖

Years later, in 1959 when my parents came to see us and their three grandchildren, we took them to the city regularly from our home in Mountain Lakes, New Jersey, thirty-two miles west of Manhattan. I remember well the day before they departed to return to Europe by ship, then the old Nieuw Amsterdam of the Holland America Line. In early afternoon, we checked them into the Plaza so that they would be a cab ride away from the pier where the ship would depart at 9:00 the following morning. Then we toured midtown in the afternoon. I thought a final view of the sprawling city of New York would befit the occasion. At that point in my dad's life we couldn't predict if he would ever be able to come back to see us. After all, he was 78 then.

Before we settled for cocktails at the Rainbow Room in Rockefeller Center, where my office was located anyway, we suggested the top observation area for a view of the city from some fifty floors above busy Avenue of the Americas. The day was clear and beautiful. Dad and Mom paused on all sides, looking around, but spent the longest time looking north, to Grand Central Park and beyond.

Then Dad started to talk, to tell us by pointing to Fifth Avenue where he was born and what he remembered of his childhood years. After that, his eyes swept over to the northwest side and I told him: "See Dad, there is Lincoln Center. The new Metropolitan Opera is there, and concert halls, and theaters."

Quiet at first, Dad looked up, then started to tell us what was there seventy-eight years ago.

"All of that land over there, from where you say is now Lincoln Center, to way up where I think I see the buildings of New York's Columbia University, all that land was owned by a crazy Irish farmer. His name was Robert O'Toole. He had about 500 head of cattle grazing there and there was nothing that would or could move him to sell it 'to them developers.'"

Years later, his heirs did sell all of the land, which then became the fashionable upper West Side. It took a nose dive in the sixties and seventies but is back where it used to be, in the dream and realm of the more affluent citizens of the Big Apple.

We all listened intently but, turning, I noticed that a large crowd had gathered around us to listen and witness the stories of someone who was obviously born here, who grew up over there on Fifth and 71st. It was a sensation to all, as no one else around us seemed to be a true New Yorker, as they are truly rare in New York. Dad received standing applause when we left to go to dinner downstairs.

❖

My father Arnold Wilhelm Hilger was born in New York as the couple's third child in 1882, followed three years later by another son and last child by the name of Peter Caspar, as tradition demanded. My dad grew up and went to school in the city. He spent his childhood learning English as his first language. But obviously his father taught him some German, the tongue spoken where he was born and grew up. But even after my grandparents retired to Europe, my father would converse only in English with his mother, Bertha Harriett, while he could be bilingual with his father, Peter Caspar.

His childhood was well guarded by strict parents. They never traveled much in those days. When they crossed the Hudson they would, then and now, call it "going to America." The family's summer vacations consisted of packing several footlockers for the rail trip to Atlantic City, where my grandmother and her kids spent all summer to escape the brutal heat of Manhattan. My grandfather would come down by train on weekends.

For business reasons, he would travel to Europe once a year by ship. These journeys took a minimum of two months. Crossing the Atlantic consumed more than two weeks. My grandmother in New York only knew if and how they arrived about five weeks after they left. On most of these travels he would take along one of his four children. My dad made the trip in the summer of 1892, when he was nine. He wrote numerous letters to his mom in New York, describing his impressions of Europe during these excursions. I have all of them in my possession, and much of what I am writing about here on these pages originated from Dad's letters to his mother.

To expand his flourishing import of high-quality tools from the mother company in Remscheid, my grandfather also wanted to take a business trip to San Francisco. The east-west railroad had just been connected with the golden spike in northern Utah, so there were through trains now available instead of going by ship around the southern tip of South America or, later, through the Panama Canal. But by inquiring with his insurance agency, he was told they could not insure his life west of Chicago. That was the year 1890. Not that long ago!

❖

Seventy years later, the new jets would make that distance in five and a half hours.

❖

When my dad was eighteen and ready for college, he needed to "find himself." He hired on a freighter leaving for a year-long trip around the world. His Merchant Marine title was Boiler Room Assistant Engineer 2nd Class, and he received no regular pay. Even in those days, young men had to find themselves. So this phenomenon of male adolescence was not only restricted to the hippies of the 1960s.

I am sure it worked well on him, especially after they sailed through the Suez Canal into the Red Sea, where the temperature in the boiler room reached 140 degrees Fahrenheit.

I know. I've been there. Fifty years later, I did likewise in a steel mill foundry in Chicago, in the midst of a steamy, humid Illinois summer.

That journey around the world also brought him to dock in Yokohama, Japan, a country that had opened to Westerners just a mere twenty years before. Returning to New York, he was ready for school and followed his father's desire and advice to enroll in Germany's famed Berlin University's School of Engineering.

That's where he met my Dutch mother. Her name was Emma Charlotte Luyken.

LUYKEN FOREBEARS

&

M y maternal grandfather, Carl Luyken, was born in Huize Landfort, Holland, as the youngest of ten children. When their parents passed away, his oldest brother Albert inherited the family's country home, which included some 2,000 acres of timberland and a dairy farm. It was customary in those days that primogeniture prevailed whereby the oldest always inherited the family domicile. Albert, however, was obliged to provide for his siblings, and so my grandfather Carl obtained a similar country home called Sonsfeld, not far away. Both straddled the Dutch/German border. Landfort was located in Holland near Gendringen, and Sonsfeld was situated across the border in Germany, near Anholt.

When their father died, his will stipulated that the brothers pay out their sisters. My grandfather Carl was strapped for cash and would have been forced to take a mortgage on his property. As a penny-pinching fellow—as he was—he refused to do so and sold Sonsfeld in order to satisfy his sisters. He bought a villa on the Rhine River in Boppard, where my mother was later married to my dad.

When the French occupied Germany after World War I, they seized Boppard and made grandfather's house the stately residence of their commanding general. My grandfather Carl told them he was Dutch, but they weren't interested. He couldn't stand the French anyway. He retreated back to Holland and settled in a town house near Arnhem.

Boppard was ultimately sold, with the help of my dad. Carl refused to deal with such a trivial matter. After the French vacated the premises, he never even set foot again in the stately villa on the slopes above the scenic Rhine. As a matter of fact, in his remaining seventeen years of life, he never even returned to Germany for as much as a short visit.

My mother was born in Sonsfeld. But her parents' Dutch nationality made her Dutch as well, according to *Jus Sanguinis,* Latin for "blood law," and the same law under which I was born as an American citizen. It governed most European nations at that time.

But Landfort was saved for the family—then. After all, the country home had already been in the hands of the Luykens for centuries. It started out as a moated castle at the time it was built, around 1600. "Landfort is een oud Kasteel met vier toorens van sonderlijk maaksel," wrote a chronicler about the place, meaning "Landfort is an old castle with four towers of an extraordinary appearance."

The house would be passed on to Albert's son, Albert Jr., according to the long-established family rule previously mentioned. As the oldest son, he would be next in line to inherit, keep and maintain it. But he and his Danish wife already lived there when I was a teenager. They occupied a small apartment in one of the wings. With some thirty-two rooms, the house was big enough for everyone.

Their twin sons were my age. Pardon, I was older than they were—I would rub that in at any opportune time—five months and one day older. They were born ten minutes apart. Albert first, then Johann. Nobody called them by those names, though. They were Abbi and Jobbi to everyone. They were my closest buddies at the time. And still are.

When I was in my early teens I spent many summer vacations in

Landfort. I would be there for at least two months. The twins and I were an inseparable trio. We were also into everything, probably a pest to Uncle Albert Senior and Uncle Albert Junior. But old Aunt Bars—Albert Senior's wife of some fifty years and the undisputed lady of the house—would hug us often, give us candy and chocolate and call us "shratteboutche" translating to "darling." She was Abbi and Jobbi's grandmother. But since I never knew my maternal grandmother Lientje, Carl's wife, I quickly adopted Aunt Bars as her substitute. It was not a difficult chore. I adored her.

As Landfort was built as a water burg in the late sixteenth century, the moat was still in place and is to this day. The entrance to the mansion's circular driveway and its stately dual front doors led across an old drawbridge. It does no longer draw open as it did four hundred years before, to protect the ancestors then living there from unwanted intruders. Opposite the drawbridge were the horse stables. In their upper floor lived Gerritt and his wife. He tended the horses and also functioned as the chauffeur, either with horse-drawn carriages or the first automobiles, which the family already owned as early as 1902.

The spacious, park-like forest and meadows surrounding Landfort, perhaps occupying some fifty acres or so of the total land belonging to it, were our vast playground. Hide and seek, pony riding, tree climbing and swimming in the Ijssel—the small river separating Holland and Germany—were our favorite pastimes day after day after day.

The pigeon tower by the moat was an especially gruesome and mysterious place for the imagination of growing boys. It was erected as high as a two-story building. The birds would use the pigeon holes arranged on the entire tower outside to slip in and build their nests. From down below, we couldn't see the critters but heard them distinctly gurgle along, probably raising their young, or mating, or both. Our imaginations would go wild with thoughts of what all these birds were doing up there.

"But where do they go to the bathroom?" I asked.

"Just take a deep breath," Abbi said and laughed.

Uncle Albert Senior had also designed a paddle-wheeler device that would fit across the heavy wooden row boat. It was anchored on each side by one heavy leather loop to hold it in place. Gerrit had built it for the twins when they were old enough to be left alone with the raft on the moat. By turning the handles of the device with our hands, the wheels on both sides would rotate and propel the boat forward. The three of us would spend hours each day circling Landfort on the moat, dreaming of present and future ventures, as all boys do.

We were close, the three of us, perhaps closer than cousins normally are. If we had an argument, a disagreement over what should be done next, there would be two against one, as is natural in a threesome, and also beneficial for any democratic decision. But while one might be inclined to think that I was always the lonely single vote because the twins were twins and would tend to think alike, that did not always occur. As often as not, one of the twins voted along with me. This custom made our being together a delight and cemented us together even more.

In Holland, lunch is a light meal, and dinner, as the main event of the day, is served early, about six in the evening. After sharpening the long carving knife over a grind stone, Uncle Albert Senior would carve the roast beef. His long-handled knife and fork had bucks' horns as handles. In doing so, slicing the meat ever so thin, his tongue would be wedged between his lips, and we knew he was not to be disturbed while performing this evening ritual.

The twins flanked him and signaled over to me, imitating their grandfather, and I, sitting next to Aunt Bars at the other end of the table, had a dickens of a time not to burst out laughing. Aunt Bars, in her great wisdom, probably knew why she had arranged the seating that way, separating the three of us. It likely served the peace and dignity of the occasion better to have us apart, far apart.

After supper, Aunt Bars would invariably entertain their house guests—who seemed to be ever present—playing chamber music in the music salon downstairs, to the left of the entrance doors. We would be asked to go upstairs, take our baths and get ready for bed.

What Aunt Bars never knew, or pretended to never know, was that we sat for hours on the upper step of the spiral staircase, to listen to a concert of Vivaldi or J.S. Bach and the grown-up chatter during intermissions. From our vantage point, we could see her sitting on the extreme forward edge of her stool in front of her piano or spinet, her Ben Franklin glasses on the tip of her nose, trying desperately to read the notes and never really succeeding because of her extreme nearsightedness.

But she knew those pieces by memory and never once stumbled across a single note. We just adored her, loved her as any grandson should.

All these happenings occurred when the world lay in its very last throes of a gracious period, when violence was not really known and when Europe had enjoyed the unprecedented period of some twenty years of peace.

My last of such summer vacations was spent in Landfort during July and August of 1939. A month later, Europe embarked on the bloody war, which was to last six years and not only destroy much of her cities but also change her way of life forever.

In the months following the Allied invasion of June 6, 1944, intense fighting rolled back and forth across Landfort. Heavy artillery fire destroyed most of the park-like grounds surrounding the mansion. Many of the centuries-old oak and beech trees fell. Most of the venerable manor house itself was shattered into a roof-less and room-less shell. Only one of the wings was intact enough for Uncle Albert Junior and his family to inhabit.

Uncle Albert Senior did not live to see the demise of Landfort. Aunt

Bars, in her upper eighties, died shortly after peace finally came in 1945.

Since I was free to roam through Europe again immediately after May 8, 1945, I set out to visit Landfort in the fall of that year. Aunt Bars was no longer alive to lend her grace to the once serene and now broken mansion. Uncle Albert Jr. was away on a trip. His Danish wife Musse, the twins' mother, refused to see me. She had always stood apart from the family, for as long as I knew her.

Abbi lived in Amsterdam. Jobbi felt crowded in the tightness of small Holland. He went to live in Monrovia, the capital of Africa's Liberia. Gerrit had aged more than the six years since I'd seen him and looked starved and thin. The pigeon tower still stood, as did one half of the mansion, although the inside was mostly ruined. The other half's roof was down. Only its outside walls remained.

Three years later, I went to study in France then went to live in the United States. I deal with this event in a later chapter. But in 1967, on a business trip to Europe when I took along my then-eleven-year-old son Peter, we detoured to Landfort to see it. Gerrit had died. Musse again refused to see us.

With the limited resources he possessed, Uncle Albert Junior had tried to rebuild Landfort. To no avail. Yet he did manage to roof the entire building, thus preventing further deterioration from the weather. But in the end, the huge taxes levied on the property in post-war—by then socialized—Holland drained all his reserves.

So in the late sixties he gave up. He offered Landfort to the Dutch government as a historic landmark under the condition that it be kept as such for centuries to come. In return, the government gave him living rights in the house, which rights were to be transferred to the oldest Luyken son of each following generation. After his father died, Abbi returned from Amsterdam and lived in the house.

The Dutch government restored most of the inside rooms, and called it officially "Huize Landfort." But to this day, the rooms are empty, void of furniture. Whatever was not destroyed during World War II, the Luykens kept.

But during the rebuilding period, the contractors found many double walls and double ceilings in the mansion. Tearing them down with the permission of Albert junior, they found genuine heavy oak beams on the higher, original ceilings and treasures behind the artificial walls of the mansion—silverware and Delft China for sixty-four guests, everything in three sizes: large dinner plates, medium lunch plates, small bread plates—then the same selections with cups, forks, knifes, spoons. Also hundreds of books still in readable print on heavy *pergament* paper were retrieved, along with old clothing that disintegrated to the touch. All of that dated back to around 1600 and was permanently donated to the Rijks Museum in Amsterdam.

Why artificial rooms in a house the size of Landfort? When the thirty-years war broke out in Europe in 1618, one of my great-great-great grandmothers had them built to hide her treasures from the marauding French and Swedes. By the time the war ended in 1648, she was long dead, and the following generations never knew about those hidden treasures.

The twins and I continued to live far apart, one in Landfort, one in Monrovia and I in North Carolina. We lost contact for the next thirty-five years.

An era had ended, never to return!

❖

My mother grew up with two sisters on Sonsfeld's sizable estate and in an impressive, mansion-like home. In spite of a multitude of servants, she was raised spartanly by her stern but loving mother Lintje, who, among other useful things, taught her to speak Dutch and German fluently.

Since the family lived way out in the country, the daughters went to school at a Catholic convent although they were Protestant. My mother would speak only Dutch with her parents and sisters. But she could easily retrieve her German to talk to a dashing bachelor from a strange, faraway country. She met him while visiting her younger sister, who was married to an architect in Berlin. Undoubtedly, their parents asked her to be Mom's chaperon.

My mom apparently fell head over heels in love with this stranger. And of course the stranger would become my dad. He was in his last semester at Berlin University's Technische Hochschule. He looked distinguished, smoked the short stubby pipe used mostly by Britons in those days and owned a twenty-eight-foot sailboat docked at Berlin's famed playground, the Wannsee. He came from an old, established, respectable family, which instantly made him acceptable by society. He proposed to her in the spring of 1913 and they married in September of that year.

But for her entire life she had a difficult time speaking English.

So these two are my parents, with a multitude of languages! Yes indeed, I grew up in a multilingual family. They were married for close to sixty years, until Dad died at almost ninety. Mom followed him eight years later, also near ninety. They were happily married, afforded us a great childhood and raised us sternly but lovingly.

When my siblings and I were young adolescents, my father would insist we speak English—mostly at dinner time on Sundays when he was at leisure and in a relaxed mood. Mom would listen for a while, then interrupt his flow of words—in German, of course—by saying that she needed to know what he planned to do the following day. And that was the end of our English for the day.

But the brain is a wonderful human instrument: I maintained a vivid memory of English throughout my childhood and until I was exposed to more of the language, first after May 1945 in communicating with

American Army and Consular personnel, then from 1949 at the Sorbonne in Paris by gaining new friendships with a lot of my American and British co-students.

My brain even stored numerous stories and descriptions about the United States and especially New York that, over time, my Dad had told. So much so that when, on my arrival in the U.S., as the *SS Argentina* approached Manhattan, I was frighteningly sure I had been there before in another life. This notion resurfaced many more times during all the following years living and traveling in our country. It seems to stay with me forever.

I came along as their fourth and last child and, although born in Germany, I was not German. German law at the time of my birth—*Jus Sanguines,* Latin for "blood law"—established citizenship by the citizenship of the child's parents. Although I was born there, that law never considered me a German National.

Both my dad and I were covered by the LEX Bancroft, which Congress passed in 1868 to unify all nationality laws existing in the various states of the U.S. The LEX Bancroft was based on the XIV Amendment to the Constitution, which in Section 1 addresses the issue of citizenship quite clearly:

"All persons born or naturalized in the United States, and subject to the jurisdiction thereof, are Citizens of the United States and the state wherein they reside. No state shall make or enforce any law which shall abridge the privileges or immunities of Citizens of the United States; nor shall any state deprive any person of life, liberty, or property, without due process of law; or deny to any person within its jurisdiction the equal protection of the laws."

Therefore I was a natural-born citizen, born in Germany to a native-born American father. That entitled me to go home to the United States anytime I wished. And believe me, that was my wish during the final war years, if I could only find my way out of Germany into Switzerland, Portugal or Sweden.

❖

During the globalization taking place in the world after WWII and with many Americans sent overseas to work, serve and therefore live abroad, their children born in foreign countries, Congress changed the laws in the early sixties to allow American citizens, including those who became citizens through immigration, to maintain dual citizenships.

❖

During the 1930s and the first few years of WWII, the Nazis had been gentle to my parents and all of us children. They knew that Dad was American born. Already before the Nazis came to power in 1933, he was shadowed off and on by the German Government Agencies. But he was gainfully employed by Siemens, a large manufacturer of electrical equipment that later became a global company. His employers made sure he was not in any way or shape bothered and made sure to give the Nazis certification that he was badly needed for the defense industry.

Dad spoke German almost without any accent. Mom had a slight but more noticeable Dutch intonation in her German, perhaps because she conversed in Dutch more frequently with her father residing near Arnhem, and her two sisters as well. I had a finely tuned ear for accents and knew very well that German was not the language my dad originally learned. He would roll the R's and do such things as pronouncing the German word for gasoline, Benzin, as we pronounce benzene, using the soft Z, instead of the hard German Z.

However, it was years after the war had ended before I found out the truth of what really happened to us during the war years in hostile Germany. It took place during a cocktail party in Washington, DC in 1950, where I met a gentleman who introduced himself by name. I did likewise, using my first name only, and asked what his occupation was. He replied he was working "for the State Department." However, when he immediately thereafter recognized my European accent and asked me questions as to where I was from, I said to him: "You are asking very specific questions, Sir. So you must be OSS? Now called CIA for Central Intelligence Agency? So you are working for the Company?"

He smiled and did not respond. But the smile and his curiosity in me gave him away. I told him my story—abbreviated. Yet when he asked, then heard my last name, he said: "I remember your name. I read it in the files we found in Berlin in 1945. Was your father's first name Arnold?"

"Yes indeed. But what did the files indicate?"

"They stated, among many other facts associated with the Hitler regime, that after Pearl Harbor your parents were required to report to the authorities once a day. But apparently your parents were so well known in the small village where you lived that it sufficed that your baker knew about your whereabouts. So the Nazis appointed him to supervise you, which was easy because he brought fresh rolls to your front door every morning. His name was Franz Gutzen; I remember that now. He was the one who shadowed you."

That piece of information triggered my mind into thinking that our mail carrier might have also checked us out, although my CIA friend didn't know anything about him. Yet I remember Mom telling me that he always seemed to know what was in my letters to her, because when he delivered the mail, he would tell her that she had a letter from her son at school in Freiburg and he was well and learning. He had obviously read my scribbles in detail.

CHILDHOOD IN EUROPE

꧁꧂

I was born in a brownstone townhouse on the outskirts of Düesseldorf, in Germany's western provinces on the left bank of the Rhine River. It was 1923 and the country's old WWI Reichsmark currency was in a wild spin of inflation. People rushed to the grocery store on payday to buy foodstuff, as ten minutes later the currency had dropped in value in another huge percentage.

The cost of my birth was over 13 million Reichsmark, equal to $25.00. I was an expensive fourth child.

The townhouse was spacious, on a quiet side street, with three stories and one etage in the attic, affording ample room for the family of six and the servants, so much so that one large room on the third floor, which had huge windows facing north, was rented out to a painter. Adjacent to his *Atelier*, as such art studios were called in French and German, our playroom occupied a similarly large space.

The painter could never pay his rent. So when I was born, he painted an oil depicting the Dutch countryside, in honor of my mother's Dutch heritage. The painting still hangs in my house. In 1925, he painted another one, in recognition of his free-rent status in our house. This one was a full-length life-sized color pencil-drawn painting of a little boy reaching up to a table where his toy trains were laid out, with a dripping piece of chocolate in his other hand. He wore the outsized shoes of his older sister. It was the beginning of the Great Depression. And his eyes were light blue and his hair was red, fire-engine red.

That was me! That work of art also hangs in my house. I banned it to the front entrance behind the front door which, when opened, would cover it. I am so embarrassed when people see it. (Yet the ladies seem to love it.)

My first live remembrance of my childhood was when after lunch—the main meal of the day in Germany—my nanny would come into the dining room to pick me up and take me upstairs for a nap. I would willingly go, carried in her arms, but only if I was given my customary banana, which I would shoulder like a civil war Confederate soldier would his rifle. "Banna," I would say. I think I was two years old. I still eat a banana a day.

At age four, I came down with a nasty infection of one of my ribs. At the *Heerdter Krankenhaus* nearby, a piece was excised from my back. The post-operative treatment consisted of one trip to the operating room every day to get the pus out of the wound. For this my parents had given me a trumpet to blow. It would cause that stuff to exit the wound and still keep it open. The operating room was on the hospital's fourth floor and overlooked the Rhine. I was fascinated by all the ships I saw.

When I turned six, we moved to another house in the country. I was enrolled in elementary school in the nearby village. The year was 1929. One day that summer I came home and walked across the lawn to the patio, where my parents had tea under a huge roll-away canvas marquee, and I called out to them *"Deutschland verrecke!"* That meant "Germany Die." I had picked up the slogan in school. It was the official greeting of the Communist Party. I think that was the first time my dad and I had a somewhat serious discussion.

A year later, at the ripe age of seven, I fell in love.

My mom had just bought me my first pair of knickerbockers, those bulky-leg things that were fashionable in England at that time. They were tied to your leg below the knee. They had no belt loops. You had to use colorful suspenders to keep them up around your waist. Mine were bright red. You also had to wear socks that came up to the lower edge of the knee joint, to your knee cap.

Shortly thereafter, I met Ingrid. She was six. She lived five houses up the street from us. She was marvelous, very pretty, I thought. She had blonde hair in braids and blue eyes. She had set my head spinning. One day, I dressed in my new, grey knickerbockers, attached the red suspenders, took my most preferred shirt out of the drawer, pranced downstairs, "borrowed" one of the many caps Dad wore, especially when he had the car's top down, and took out his cane kept in a tall vase by the entrance and used on walks in the forest nearby.

Then I strode up to Ingrid's house, swinging the cane as I had seen Dad do, whistled a song and thought I looked debonair enough to call on the young lady of my choice. Unbeknownst to me, all the neighbors, and my parents as well, watched me with great smiles on their faces. The disaster came when I rang her doorbell then asked her mother for her.

"She is upstairs. I'll call her."

"I can go upstairs."

"No, you wait here."

Ingrid was aloof that morning. She didn't even notice my new knickerbockers. It all turned out to be such a colossal fiasco, the end of my first love affair. But a lasting memory, nonetheless.

Once a week, a four-wheel, canvas-covered wagon drawn by two horses rumbled up to the house. Muscular helpers with big beer bellies unloaded long, rectangular ice blocks and brought them to our ice chest in the basement. Those big guys lugging ice chunks scared me out of my senses.

For some reason, I thought they would harm me.

On a brighter note, *Frau Weihselbaeumer* came around every morning with her one-horse-drawn milk cart. Our servants would run outside to have our cans filled with milk fresh from the cows. We often helped her. Our reward was to ride with her on top of her wagon to the farm, where we were allowed to see the other animals in their stables: cows, sheep, goats, chicken.

Also every morning, our village baker, *Herr Franz Gutzen*, brought us our fresh rolls. Some twenty years later, his name resurfaced in my life, and, as mentioned before, I learned what I couldn't even have guessed when I was a young boy.

My school pals and I often went to the forest near our house. In remote parts we built "fortresses" with camouflaged walkways to the fire roads. On the way through the thickets, we would lie on the ground to watch young couples who regularly came to the woods. They would kiss, lie on the pine needles on the soft forest floor and move in strange rhythmical ways that we could not understand. Sometimes they locked and cried out as if they were fighting. But then they kissed again. "What's all this for?" we asked. It was strange to us. And funny!

December 6 was always a special day. St. Nicolas Day. On the evening of the fifth, we would place a plate with sugar lumps on the sill below an open window. Sugar? "For St. Nicolas's horse," Mom would say. "He is hungry and needs to eat."

The next morning the plate would normally be full of cookies and chocolate. But once I got a wooden whip instead from Nick. Nothing else. "It's because you were not behaving well. He knew that," Dad muttered. I was sad but knew it was true. What I never knew until many years later was that his heart was heavy with sorrow and guilt.

At age eight, I met the last German *Kaiser*, Wilhelm Viktor Albert. At Germany's loss of WWI in November 1918, he was convinced by the then five-star general Paul Von Hindenburg, commander of all Royal Armed Forces of Germany, that the monarchy was over and the time for a republic had begun. That meant exile for the Kaiser. He abdicated his throne in Berlin and was escorted to Holland, where the Dutch royal family offered him one of their castles at Doorn as his permanent domicile. His official names and titles were: Kaiser Wilhelm II of Germany, King Wilhelm of Prussia and Prince Wilhelm Viktor Albert von Hohenzollern. He was the last of the long line of *Kaisers* and kings the royal family of Germany had contributed to the House of Prussia during the almost 500 years since it was formed by the first prince.

Wilhelm II had ruled Germany for thirty years.

I don't quite remember the day I met the Kaiser. It must have been during my summer vacations with my grandfather Carl Luyken in Holland. One day he asked me: Grandson, would you like to meet the *Kaiser?*"

"Okay. Who is he?"

My grandfather explained. I had no idea what a Kaiser was or what he was supposed to do. But anyway, I loved my grandfather and decided that surely he knew why I should meet this fellow. In his brand new 1934 Ford V8 we drove over to Doorn, where I was introduced to the *Kaiser*. He looked like my grandfather: the same haircut, the same goatee, the same height. They could easily have been brothers.

I also found out they were almost the same age and were both enthusiastic wood carvers. As a matter of fact, years later my grandfather took a large piece of oak out of his supply room and carved out of it a replica of the Hohenzollern Burg in Sigmaringen, about twenty inches long and six to eight inches high. The *Kaiser's* family returned it to my mother shortly after the former ruler of Germany died in 1941.

Other than that, I was not much impressed with the Kaiser but more interested in all the gold and silver he had standing around in his large house. Another relic was an old bicycle; already then was I a bicycle nut! I loved that old bike. It had a super large front and extremely small rear wheel. Funny looking.

On the way home my grandfather asked: "How did you like the *Kaiser?*"

"Well, he seemed an okay guy but I was disappointed. I thought all Kaisers and Kings sit on a throne. He didn't. He wasn't even dressed like I thought a Kaiser should be. But I guess that's the way *Kaisers* do it."

Not much happened during the next two years in school. At the beginning of the third year, 1933, I entered high school, "Gymnasium" as it was called in Germany. From textbooks of the time, heavily censored and re-written to suit the dogma of the Nazi regime, we learned most of the events in German history that had any resemblance to the philosophies of Hitler. Karl the Great, Napoleon conquering Russia (the defeated part was omitted), Caesar (what he did in Rome and not what he did to conquer the *Germanen),* the last Kaiser Wilhelm II (omitting his relationships to the Russian Czar and Queen Victoria) and the great personalities that ruled Germany with an iron fist for the so-called "benefit" of the populace. On the sideline, heroes of Spain and ruthless rulers of Italy were also mentioned. Japanese heritage was mostly left out; was it perhaps that the German Education Ministry didn't know anything about the Far East? Or if so, did it not fit the Hitler image? Was it perhaps too brutal even for a brutal dictator of his sort?

The high school was named after the late past President and Field Marshal Paul Von Hindenburg.

My first memorable experience there was one of my teachers smacking my face twice with the flat back of his right hand. He was not happy with what I did or said. I don't remember why. But what I do remember is that blood gushed out of both nostrils at a constant and unstoppable rate. My parents were notified and rushed to school from wherever they were, but an ambulance had already taken me to a hospital.

I heard later that they had a quite frank, open talk with the principal that left no doubt as to what they were thinking about the teacher clobbering me. I was elated. Vindication! The man never argued with me for the rest of that school year. He had learned his lesson the hard way.

I went to Holland that next summer, to be with my cousins in Landfort. That was always a great treat.

When I was twelve and in my third year at high school—"Quarta" it was called in Germany—I had a rapid succession of severe mishaps with my right knee. First, someone kicking a ball during soccer practice hit the inside of my knee full force. It knocked out the meniscus, those precious cushions the body provides in the knee, between the upper and lower part of the leg. That winter I broke down again skiing and the following summer, a bicycling trip through Bavaria did the rest. I spent eight months in hospitals and rehabilitation centers, to no avail. I slipped down one grade in school because I missed an entire school year.

My knee was shattered for good. It is fused now and has been for all these years. But when I finally came home, the first thing I did the following morning was look for my bicycle in the garage. I pulled it out, pumped up the tires and was trying to mount it by swinging my now stiff leg over the saddle when Mom saw me through the kitchen window. "NO," she hollered. But I was in the saddle then and pedaled away, one leg hanging down, the other one pedaling.

"Bye, Mom," I hollered back.

She called the surgeon who had treated me all these months.

"Let him," he said. "He wants to be like his peers. It's good for him."

All of this did not stop me from taking a summer job on weekends. A farmer nearby owned a lot of ponies. He had a contract with a fashionable and much frequented restaurant in the next village. My job was to guide ride-on-back tours for visiting kids, on the farmer's ponies. He employed us village boys to do the dressing of the animals, ride them to the restaurant, guide the tours all day, ride the ponies back, hose them down, brush them, give them water from a bucket and feed them, then ride our bikes back home. The farmer did not pay us nearly as much as we were making in tips. Not a bad deal, we thought.

When I was in sixth grade—"Unter Sekunda" it is called in the German school system—I met Helmut. He attended high school as I did. It turned out to be a milestone in my life. We were both in our mid-teens. I was taller than he, but he packed more muscles on his broad frame. He had dark brown hair with brown eyes almost the same color. I was red-haired, blue-eyed and freckled.

Going from class to class, we saw each other often. He looked interesting to me, kind of outdoorsy. Sometime later during this period when we crossed the halls, I nodded. So did he. Soon thereafter we talked to each other. But we had different sets of friends in school with whom we would hang out. So I did not see or speak to him at length until the following year.

That was when I found out he was an experienced kayaker. He didn't tell me that, but I watched him in action that summer of 1938. He participated in a kayak event in Bavaria where I happened to be vacationing with my folks. On a white water stretch near Fuessen where we stayed, I witnessed his expertise in negotiating tight spots and thundering water cascades. I knew then that he was a master of the sport even at his early age. Some years before, I had begun to be interested in kayaking myself but never became experienced in the sport. So here was Helmut, a classmate, so to speak, even though he was older. He was seventeen, I fifteen. To teenagers, two years make a lot of difference!

Right then, after the event, I went over to him after he had beached his kayak at the finish line and congratulated him on his run. He grinned. "It was fun. You should try it some time."

"I would LOVE to," I instantly blurted out.

"Good. When we get home, I'll show you a few moves and tricks. The first thing you'll have to learn is the roll."

"What's that?"

"We call it a 360. It means you have to roll the kayak once around through the water to learn to come up again."

"Okay, got that. What then?"

"Then I'll show you your best paddling position, stuff like that. We'll go out on the Rhine first, to give you an introduction. We can take a smaller, faster river after that."

I was in seventh heaven.

Soon after we returned home, we went out in his two-seat sea kayak. They were quite a bit wider than white-water kayaks. He taught me my sitting position, my forward stroke with each side of the paddle. He showed me how to handle currents, especially around the river's numerous jetties. He guided me through some of the rapids.

In October, my dad found an inexpensive used kayak made out of wood. I needed—and built myself with Helmut's help—a two-wheeled cart to roll it to the river some three kilometers one way. Weighing a ton, or so it felt, it was nevertheless a good tool to learn on.

By fall, I had learned a lot about the sport!

By fall, I had my own sea kayak. When we went out, we each had our own!

By fall, we had become kayaking buddies!

Realizing that I was hooked onto a new sport—and likely also wholeheartedly approving of their son's new friendship—my parents gave me a new Klepper single canvas-type kayak like Helmut's for Christmas that year. Narrow, sleek and fast, they were made for white-water rivers. They were equipped with a spray skirt to prevent the water from entering the kayak in a roll. Helmut's rig was faded green and well used. Mine was brand new and still dark green in color.

During the winter, we often got together after school, walked down to the river, talked about kayaking and dreamt about next spring when we could go out again.

The following summer of 1939, we set out together for almost three weeks of kayaking white water rivers in the European Alps. I was still a minor at sixteen and needed the permission of my parents. But they had met Helmut. By then, he was a frequent visitor to our home. My folks approved of him.

Both kayaks could be folded into a backpack and checked on the train. At the river, we assembled them in about twenty minutes. They were light enough to be shouldered in portage areas. In contrast to today's white-water kayaks, they also had storage space for camping gear and food.

Helmut taught me white-water kayaking that summer—the REAL stuff! He was superb in handling his rig. It showed his great expertise but also outstanding courage and sometimes daredevilness. He was a master. But with me, he was always cautious and concerned for my safety. He would not allow me to do the things he did until he felt sure I could master them.

I learned my first rolls in real surroundings; I learned to negotiate the rapids around great boulders and through cascading masses of water without needing to roll. And when I finally achieved the necessary skills, he led me down the next river at full speed, both of us screaming in joy when we had negotiated the tight spots or wild rapids, then laughing all the way to the next one.

At night we would find a spot on the river's edge and set up our tent. We always picked locations near a village so we could climb up the river bank and walk to a nearby eatery for grub and beer—lots of beer, usually the dark stuff. And nobody asked us for our ID to see if we were eighteen. Which we weren't.

After that we would sit in front of our tent, listen to the water burble past, and talk endlessly about our lives, about girls and—forever—about the sport of kayaking.

We also made plans for our next trip together the following summer after Helmut had graduated and before he was to enroll in the University at Munich.

That never happened. We were home again from our journey down the fast rivers in late August. Hitler invaded Poland on September first. WWII had started.

Two months later, Helmut was drafted into Hitler's Wehrmacht. Another month later, in December, he was hit near Warsaw by a Russian-made hand grenade. He didn't live long enough to be home for another Christmas.

Eighteen years old!

Knowing him, his outstanding courage, his sense of duty, he probably went beyond the limits to serve his fatherland. His death created a void in me, a huge void! I was only sixteen. He had been my role model. I had wanted to be like him in my life. I'm convinced our friendship would have lasted well into our adult lives as so many others did.

The next two summers while I was still home, I went to the river often, alone, either sitting on my favorite jetty when it was too cold or in my kayak when it turned warmer. The war went on, became more vicious and ultimately ended in chaos.

❖

During subsequent post-war years at universities in Germany and France, I found no time or chance to kayak. Then I married, we moved to the U.S. and I became a father. Hanna thought the sport might be a bit too risky for the head of household. So I gave it up.

But in 1985 when Hanna was in Europe and our children long grown up, I had a chance to kayak twenty-two miles down the Green River Canyon Gorge in Utah in a rented super-light fiberglass rig.

The rapids were not wild that day but just curly enough to pump up my adrenalin. I screamed in joy—yippee!—and a few seconds later the canyon echoed my yippee-yippee joyous outburst. To me the sound seemed to be familiar. Was it Helmut's voice answering? Was it the screaming of the two of us when we sped down some European rivers so many decades ago?

I was sure it was. My thoughts were intensely with him then. And always it seemed that he was there with me!

❖

In May 1942, I graduated from Düsseldorf's Hindenburg Gymnasium.

My small cat-whisker radio was still my link to the world. Almost every evening between 11:00 pm and midnight, I listened intensely to the BBC newscast on short waves through the headsets of my crystal radio set, hidden deep under my pillow.

Lebensbornheime flourished. To perpetuate the 1,000-year Reich, lots of blond, blue-eyed kids were born out of wedlock in these institutions. Hitler had conquered Europe. The Wehrmacht stood at Moscow's western edge. Goebbels demanded German victory over the world and threatened to destroy Judaism to its roots. In a two-hour speech in Hamburg, he hollered into the microphone: *"Deutsche Volksgenossen, wollt Ihr den totalen Krieg?"* (German comrades, do you want a total war?)

"JAAAAA," thousands of voices roared.

Yet, he hadn't asked me.

Most of my classmates were instantly drafted into the Armed Forces. Through the *Arbeitsdienst* (Compulsory Labor Service), the regime had the names of everybody between the ages of sixteen and twenty. They could draw on them at will for serving in the *Wehrmacht, Marine und Luftwaffe* (The Armed Forces).

❖

Two years later, at the end of 1944, my wife's older brother was drafted into the Wehrmacht. It had run out of uniforms to issue, so he wore civilian clothes.

Assigned to man an anti-aircraft gun that did not work properly anymore, he was given a rifle to shoot at low-flying Allied fighters. The Germans were— by then—severely decimated and needed every hand they could find. He was only fifteen years old.

❖

The ghettoes of Warsaw and the Baltic States had been emptied, the Jews either caught and imprisoned in *Konzentrationslagern* (concentration camps) or already murdered. Few escaped into Holland or even England. Those few fortunate escapees managed to emigrate later to the United States.

Another few were lucky enough to escape—undetected by the German border guards—to Switzerland, then fly to Lisbon for the crossing of the Atlantic. But at that time, the only airline flying from Zürich to Portugal was Lufthansa, Germany's National Carrier. Consequently, Hitler quickly put an end to that "leak" by asking everyone flying that route to surrender their passports. He could then catch everyone with a Jewish name, to bring them back to Germany into the camps, and a sure death.

Yet, Hitler feared bad propaganda from his pursuit of them and therefore ordered one of the camps, Bergen Belsen, to be a public showcase for the seven other murder factories. It was hidden deep in the *Lüneberger Heide,* a large and mostly uninhabited area of heather growth south of Hamburg. It held only well cleaned, well dressed and well fed inmates ordered to smile when foreign visitors of the press came to inspect.

Meanwhile, German U-Boats had appeared along the U.S. East Coast and along the Keys of Florida. The country submitted to strict rationing as her shipyards and factories began to produce a flood of weapons, Jeep four-wheel drive vehicles, Liberty freighters and B-17 bombers. Their impact on the war would soon thereafter be felt by the Nazi regime in Germany.

In 1942, Hitler's power and terror over Europe had reached its peak.

I had heard it all from London's BBC news. If detected, I could have been arrested for treason and instantly killed in a concentration camp. But I was never caught.

Since the entry of the United States into the war after Pearl Harbor, I had successfully avoided referring to my foreign status in public. By the law of the country, I could have easily been drafted. Hitler needed every man he could get. But in retrospect, I blessed my accident when I was twelve that left me with a fused right leg. That "infirmity" saved me from the draft. My two brothers, however, were not that fortunate.

In the fall of that year, I left home, took my precious possession—the radio—with me and enrolled in medical school at the University of Freiburg.

I was nineteen years of age.

AS STUDENT AT THE UNIVERSITY OF FREIBURG

⚜

In 1943, one year later, I ran across the Kaiser's grand-nephew Fritz von Hohenzollern. His German title was *Erbprinz*—"Crown Prince" in English—because his father, Fürst Friederich, was still alive. Fritz, as the oldest son, would inherit the title when his father closed his eyes. I was not a prince. I was not even aristocratic. I was a commoner. And I still am. Yet Fritz and I became inseparable friends.

Here is the story of how that happened:

Fritz and I met in school, at the University of Freiburg, Germany, during its winter 1943/44 semester. He was enrolled in his first semester of economics, I in my third semester in medical school. We virtually ran into each other rounding a corner in Freiburg university's central auditorium.

The school was officially called Ludovica Albertina University. It was founded in 1457 by Albert IV, Archduke of Austria. Nowadays it is best reputed for the excellence of its faculties of medicine and law. I spent six years there. It was my first and foremost Alma Mater. Graduate school followed later, at the University of Paris, La Sorbonne. It became my second Alma Mater.

Freiburg is an old town. Located at the foot of the Black Forest's western slope, forty kilometers north of Basel, Switzerland, and twenty-one kilometers east of the Rhine River, it was declared a "free town" in 1120. *Freistadt*, as it is called in German, meant independence from the reigns of either the church or any dukes and kings. It meant self-government.

But in 1219 it fell back into the hands of the rulers of Urach, where it stayed until 1366, when the city again purchased its freedom. Unable to reimburse its creditors two years later, it was obliged to recognize the supremacy of the House of Hapsburg. That is where it remained until the Austrian Empire collapsed.

The small river *Dreisam* flows down from the mountains of the Black Forest and passes the city on its southern outskirts. But during the early stages—sometime in the fifteen-hundreds—the city fathers channelled some of the clear mountain water through the streets of Freiburg. They built narrow stone ditches, barely a foot wide and a foot deep, between road pavement of cobblestones and sidewalks of wooden planks—both replaced today by more modern building techniques—for the water to run down to eventually rejoin the river. The stone ditches were never replaced as far as anyone can remember, just maintained in good order over all these years.

This always-fresh water also feeds all of the city's fountains, of which there are many. The system is intact and working perfectly to this day.

Apart from the necessities of learning, students found Freiburg a "heaven." To the east, Hinterzarten and Triberg, with the adjacent highest mountain of the Black Forest, the *Feldberg*, were a forty-five-minute train ride away. The area provided excellent skiing in the winter. The train snaked up there through the *Hoellental*—"Hell Valley" in English—which derived its name from the sheer rock walls and cascading waters of the *Dreisam*. Along with the highway and double tracks of the railroad, the river squeezed through the pass's tight spaces like a thread through a sewing needle's eye.

To the west, the *Kaiserstuhl*—"emperor chair" in English—a string of moderately high hills, offered beauty, hiking trails and vineyards in great numbers. Its wine was excellent, but to this day it is primarily consumed only locally. The vintners always maintained that it did not "travel" well, so students and natives pitched in and drank great quantities right there.

The climate was mild and mellow in town, yet wintry in the mountains. A stately opera house was located opposite the university auditorium. During the winter it served as a theater as well. It presented a good repertoire of operas, operettas, well-rehearsed plays and concerts. But during the summer months, many of the performances were held outside on the cobblestone plaza surrounding the *Münster*. This magnificent cathedral was built between 1122 and 1252, using red sandstone materials. The church has only one spire. It provided a memorable backdrop for more serious plays and classical music such as the somber and tragic rendering of Brahms' *Requiem*.

For the thirsty and hungry scholar, the city had available an abundance of beer cellars, wine rooms, sidewalk cafes, brauhauses and other rustic eateries.

Before summer recess began, a bunch of guys—nine of us, including the aristocratic Fritz—had spent the night drinking beer in the cellar of the old *Rathaus*, the "house of counsel" in a true translation of this German word. Built in 1235, it was the sandstone city hall, with religious paintings adorning its side walls. It stood right opposite the tall, gothic cathedral as it has done for centuries.

But we students weren't that much intrigued with all that history. What did interest us was the fact that in its cellar, the *Rathaus* had a tavern. It was a befitting place for the purpose of good-natured get-togethers with pals devoted to having a good time. It was cool and rustic, with wine barrels lining the rock walls, and the heavy smell of fermentation in the air.

We had consumed a fair share of spirits when, at three in the morning, the place closed down for the night. We were then "encouraged" to leave. Well, we did. We headed home to our quarters, walking north on the city's main street. It was a starry, mellow and warm night in June.

Then one of us came up with the thought to take off our shoes and socks and walk barefoot in those little riverbeds which ran in cemented ditches between road and sidewalk. They surely would cool us down, we thought, physically and in our fogged minds. With a great amount of howling, we followed this great idea, marching single file through the ice-cold river water with our shoes and socks in hand!

Thus we arrived at a fairly large fountain. It was a monument well known to us, dating back to earlier times. When the Dukes of Baden— then the state of which Freiburg was the capital—needed to document their power and status, they built mansions, fountains and other expressions of wealth. This fountain was such a creation. It featured several oversized statues of men with sinister faces and long beards, standing legs spread and holding monumental swords, guarding the doings of the citizenry below.

But at fifteen past three in the morning, none of that was on our minds. We all had seen these old men on top of the fountain before. They did not bother us now, with our feet nice and cool. So we decided to rip off all our clothes, drop them on the mosaic sidewalk and go swimming in the fountain's bubbling water. Loudly carousing as we had done since leaving the tavern, we chanted student songs and whatever else came to mind. Anything any of us ever said seemed very funny and caused roars of laughter.

Alas, we heard the sirens. Warning of an approaching air raid? No, police cruiser sirens! The sound penetrated even our beer-fogged minds.

We tried to bolt out of the water but had no time left to escape, grab our clothes, get dressed and run. So we stood, all nine of us, stark naked, motionless, trying to pass as part of the fountain's mighty statues depicting some distant water god or goddess.

And so we hoped for the best. But naturally, in our condition, with that many liters of beer aboard, no one could stand motionless for very long. The Polizei knew at once what went on. We were taken to the station and fined one mark each, then freed to go home. At ten the next morning, headachy and hung-over, we paid the fine, as we had been told, in the same police station. We had chosen to pay in *Pfennig*, all nine of us, slowly counting them out individually on the policemen's desks, nine hundred pennies in all!

"Get out of here, fast," they called after us when we were done and started to bolt out of the station, "and BEHAVE!"

THE NUNS OF ST. DOMINICUS

◆

In June of 1944, we readied for the long summer recess. Fritz went back to his parents' residence, the well-known Hohenzollernburg near Sigmaringen. I headed north to a Dominican-run hospital in Heerdt to fulfill my obligation to work the better part of my summer recess as an orderly as the rules in med school required.

One week I was scheduled for twelve-hour shifts during the day, 7:00 to 7:00, and the next week during the night, 7:00 to 7:00. I lived with my parents and labored eight kilometers away at the *Heerdter Krankenhaus*, the very same where I was operated on for a rib removal in 1927.

Situated at the banks of the Rhine River, the hospital was owned, run and staffed solely by nuns. On day-shift weeks, I slept at home, while on night-shift weeks I was assigned a small, sparsely furnished but very clean bedroom in the employee section of the compound, situated in its lush vegetable and fruit gardens. Nuns in full regalia but bare feet would work there from daybreak to sundown to plow, pull the weeds, gather the fruits of Mother Earth, plant young seedlings or re-seed. Intermittently but regularly, they would briefly pause to pray by the statue of Maria and her child.

Commuting was either by *de Fitz* (bicycle) on sunny days or by two connecting tram lines when the weather was inclement.

My duties included rolling patients around the hospital on a gurney, preparing them for surgery, being present at the entire time of their surgery, bringing them back to their station, making beds, servicing bedpans, cutting patients' finger- and toe-nails, clipping their hair, assisting male patients with bathing, and doing everything else the nuns had no time to do.

I worked well with the nuns. They were kind to me, never ordered me around, never acted mean at all. I liked sister Elmira the best. As much as I could detect, she was still very young, a novice in the order. She still wore her hood in starched white. The older nuns wore black. Most of them on the hospital floors were trained nurses. They would never notice me when I pushed an empty gurney around from one room back to the station. But if sister Elmira would be headed the same way I was going, I often offered her a ride. She would hop on the flat bed of the roller, sit sideways as ladies used to do when riding horses, and laugh out loud when I hit a sharp corner to get around into the main section of the hospital. Her wide skirt, along with her legs, would then fly up high. And she would scream with joy.

The nuns obviously liked me. They called me *Schratboutje*, the Dutch name for darling. "You are so cute," Elmira would call out when I answered a summons to a room to lift a patient onto the gurney for a trip to the OR. "I love your freckles," she would add when, to my amazement, she tussled my red locks.

Mother Superior must have gotten wind of that, because she came to me one day and said: "No hanky-panky here, son. You will remember your manners, right?"

"Yes, Ma'am."

"It's not 'Ma'am,' it's 'Mother Superior.'"

"Yes, Mother."

Then she would graciously glide away. She looked and acted aristocratic. She was definitely more refined in her face and speech compared to the sisters working the large vegetable garden outside my quarters. They appeared to have originally come from the dairy farms.

Maybe, I mused, I could find out what Mother Superior looked like if I ever had to wheel her on a gurney into the X-Ray or OR. This was a possibility because when I picked them up in their quarters they did not wear their gear. They wore night gowns. Yes, you read it right: I picked them up in their cells.

My duties also included retrieving the nuns, when they were sick, from their Spartan bedrooms on the third floor. Females were not allowed up there. Only male doctors and male orderlies were. Sister Elmira told me so. Those were their rules, not ours.

Their cells were so small and narrow that I could not bring the gurney in alongside their bunks. I had to leave it in the equally narrow hallway and carry a nun to it from her *pritche*, as the narrow bunk was called. When I did, I would ask the nuns as I did the patients: "Sling your arms around my neck." I had learned it was then much easier to lift them because it meant less dead weight.

One time I asked sister Elmira: "What do you wear when you take your weekly bath?"

She laughed and said: "We are not allowed to see ourselves naked so we wear long shirts reaching to our feet."

"But how can you soap that way?"

She smiled but did not reply. And I knew then that I had gone too far. But the next time she sat on my gurney for a ride to room 28, I noticed her golden ring band on her right hand. So I asked: "Are you married?"

She laughed and smiled again when she answered: "Yes, I am married to Jesus."

Then I asked no more. All of this turned out to be another learning curve for the twenty-one-year-old, red-haired and freckled orderly, who was so utterly naïve and obviously well sheltered during his childhood.

I had not known much about the sisters of St. Dominicus before that summer, but I had now developed a sincere, deep respect for their selfless life devoted solely to serving others.

❖

In April 2008, during a trip to the Netherlands, I passed the hospital briefly, slowed down, turned the rental car around and went closer to see it. But I could not find its solid dark-red brick walls. A park now stood where the hospital had been so many moons ago. And on its former river side stood a new high-rise hospital which looked much more up-to-date and modern but somehow lacked the familiar and friendly ambience of the old. At least its front entrance was adorned with a sign: "Dominican Hospital."

The gardens were still there but no longer cultivated for growing food for the nuns. Instead, they were turned into green grass. And I was sure I could detect the edge of a small house in there, the one where I lived when I was on duty.

A LONDON BLITZ

The fourth semester at medical school in Freiburg had concluded in May 1944. The fifth semester was scheduled to start in October '44 and to end at Christmas with the *Physikum*, the German designation for completion of all first-stage medical requirements in physiology, non-organic and organic chemistry and—foremost—anatomy, which included two winter courses in dissection of the human body for both muscle and nerve structures.

At all times, both at home and in the hospital compound during that summer, I had my shortwave radio with me. I would never be without it. I used it every day to be up on the news in the world. I carried it with me in an inconspicuous, thirty-year-old backpack with frayed edges.

One evening when I was off shift at seven and at home in my room, I went to bed shortly before ten and, as was my habit, attached the earphones to my head under my pillow. I fumbled with the cat whisker. It always had to be in the right space on the crystal to link up with the BBC in London. That process consumed a few minutes as I tried to obtain the maximum clarity and volume. Having achieved this, I heard the anchor man Malcolm say: "When the first flying bombs crossed the Channel around the middle of June 1944, the riddle of what concrete truth, if any, there was behind all these rumors, seemed solved."

I strained my ears. What in the world was he talking about? I wanted to be sure to hear the entire story. But sometimes atmospheric disturbances made that impossible. I fooled around again with the cat whisker and a minute later heard Malcolm explain: "Soon thereafter, on July 6, 1944, Winston Churchill spoke of an up-to-then completely unknown place called Peenemuende as the "main experiment station both of the flying bomb and the long-range rocket."

After a short interruption caused by my trying to find a better spot on the crystal, I heard him add: "At first our information led us to believe that a rocket weapon would be used. This made it the truth that indeed there was a German long-range rocket."

I heard my parents downstairs readying to retire for the night. So I switched Malcolm off by putting the headset down and straightened out my blanket and pillow, just in case Mom would come in and check on me. She did, tiptoed to my bed, felt the bulb in my night stand lamp as she had always done and said in no uncertain terms: "I thought you are on duty at seven tomorrow morning and wanted to go to sleep at ten. It's almost midnight. What were you doing all this time?"

"Just reading. Here, it is a fascinating book by Carl May about the Indians. Winnetou is his hero," I added quickly. I'd loved him when I was in my teens.

"Ja, I believe you. Now, go to sleep. Good night."

"Yes, good night, Mom, I will." Close call!

I was somewhat confused because during this time, roughly twice a month, there had been a sensational "disclosure" about the nature of a German "secret weapon." I remembered Malcolm's earlier hints at this subject. He also apparently had proof now of what the world obviously knew: that the British and American Press had been in the habit of referring to the French coast between Calais and Cherbourg as the "rocket-gun coast." The Germans obviously tried to hide these facts from the citizens of their conquered countries, which, by that time, was most of Europe.

The next evening he reported: "These stories are being spread by teletype to any newspaper editor who might feel inclined to print them. They usually come with a Stockholm or Zurich dateline and tell amazing things. One version had it that the new German weapon would utterly destroy an area of twenty square miles with one blow. Another report told of "tons of liquid air," that made artificial icebergs all around southern England. A third writer "knew" that the weapon was "a rocket weighing fifteen tons, which was first lifted by an airplane to a high altitude in order to increase its range."

He paused for a moment, probably to study his notes again. Then he continued his newscast: "Most of these reports contained scientific or technological absurdities; many of them also looked as if they had been planted by Dr. Göbbels' propaganda forces. But what seems certain is that these rockets are developed in a large complex of research stations in Peenemuende, situated at the Baltic Sea Coast south of Sweden."

Of course I knew Peenemuende. My parents had vacationed there at the Baltic Sea beaches when I was younger. It was a small village located at a strategic spot along the large body of water the Baltic Sea forms, jutting north on a peninsula towards the island of Rügen. As in Cape Canaveral, the distance between the rocket station and the Baltic Sea contained no inhabited land but just a bird sanctuary called *der Ruden*. That meant rockets could be launched due north straight over water—and Sweden—towards the North Pole.

Allied Intelligence knew this because, also in June 1944, a long-range rocket had been mistakenly directed toward Sweden.

"It burst apart in a fiery explosion and ended its career high over the Kalmar area," Malcolm had said on the radio that evening. "If a rocket breaks up in the air its pieces 'flutter' to the ground with reasonable gentleness, so that they are not smashed beyond recognition. The Swedes agreed to hand the pieces over to the Allies, and they have been flown to England by an American pilot."

I was exited so much that sleep escaped me that night. Will Hitler win this war with his new weapons? Do the western Allies have any weaponry to intercept these deadly, un-controllable, unmanned flying bombers? Will *Der Führer* ultimately be in charge of the whole world?

What's going to happen to me?

But the question still was whether such rockets could be used operationally. By the time Winston Churchill announced that this was the case—the first V-2 fell at 6:43 p.m., September 8, 1944, at Chiswick; the second one, sixteen seconds later at Epping—the British Air Ministry had not only completed its studies of the wreckage from Sweden but even prepared a detailed release that was carried by the British newspapers the next morning.

That night, the BBC went into a lengthy dissertation about the rocket program. Malcolm began his news hour earlier, at 10:00 pm, and made it two hours instead of the customary one, because of the amount of information that had been analyzed by the experts at the British Air Ministry. He reported: "The long-rumored 'secret weapon' turned out to be a rocket of about twelve tons take-off weight, capable of carrying a payload (warhead) of one ton over a range of approximately 200 miles. The surprising thing to the then comparatively small number of people interested in rockets was not that this had been done but how the Germans had managed to do it so fast. Countless people asked me about the size of German rockets as the Germans had known them prior to 1935. Authorities on the subject could reply only that the biggest, finished in the spring of 1933, had been about man-sized.

"In the United States meanwhile, the largest rocket, developed by Dr.

Robert H. Goddard, fired on May 31, 1935, at the Mescalero Ranch near Roswell in New Mexico—by coincidence, fairly near, as they judge distances in New Mexico, to today's White Sands Proving Ground—had been somewhat taller than the German rocket, had weighed a little less, but had reached a height of 7500 feet, while the German example had got stuck on its launching pad."

Malcolm paused for a few seconds, then interrupted his program by announcing: "Ladies and Gentlemen, I will have to go off the air. We have sirens sounding in London and we should seek shelter. I will resume when the raid is over."

I decided to get out of bed, go downstairs to the kitchen and get myself a glass of milk and two of Mom's delicious, home-baked *Spekulazius* cookies. I was wide awake. The house was quiet. Peace abounded. But I was not at peace. The news was not good for the ultimate outcome of this brutal war. How will the Allies knock this madman in Berlin off his rocker, burn him, kill him, nail him against a cross? He did not deserve any better.

Malcolm came back on the air over an hour later. I was reading a book. Our house was asleep, peaceful. But air raids had been there before as well, some mild, others fierce. Yet in typical British understated fashion, Malcolm resumed: "Well, that was close. It knocked my cup of tea off my desk. Nothing spilled, heavens forbid."

After a brief pause when I heard another voice say a few instructions in the distance, which I could not understand, Malcolm continued: "As far as their solid-fuel rockets went, the German Army researchers once more revived, with lots of internal resistance, an old tradition. Soldiers during WW II, as well as their countrymen at home, usually believed that the bomb-loaded rockets they fired—or as the public saw them fired in the newsreels—were something brand-new. They were that, but not really. In reality, it was the third era in which rockets were weapons of war.

"The first such era had begun soon after the introduction of rockets in Europe and had lasted, in round figures, from 1250 to 1400 A.D.

"The second era began at about the turn of the nineteenth century and is linked with a British captain by the name of William Congreve. He reintroduced rockets as a bomb-carrying weapon. That he was successful is shown by the simple fact that only a decade later he had been promoted to general and was knighted Sir William Congreve. This second era, however, lasted barely half a century.

"Ladies and Gentlemen, this will conclude tonight's broadcast. I wish you a pleasant, peaceful and restful night and will resume my news hour tomorrow at the usual time."

I was off duty at the hospital the next morning, so I went to the bookshelves in my parents' home to look for the encyclopedia, published in 1938 by the then well known German *Brockhaus Verlag*. And I found quite a bit of information on rockets existing up to that time. Mass production would likely become possible in any future war, the article said, because by then propelling charges would have been developed, which were considered to be the basis for assembly-line manufacture. Although the chemistry of these charges was not the same on both sides of the Atlantic nor were the methods of mass production, they could nevertheless all be produced.

As far as liquid-fuel rockets were concerned, I continued reading in the rocket section of the *Brockhaus*, the German research stations at Kummersdorf West, and later Peenemunde, had little "former art," as the patent law calls it, to go by. But there was a scientific background. In the early days of the twentieth century, a Russian high-school teacher, Konstantin E. Ziolkovsky, began to write about rockets of a large size, possibly man-carrying and intended for liquid fuels. His ideas were among the earliest, but they remained unknown outside of Russia.

Then just after the first world war, in 1920, the American physicist

Professor Robert H. Goddard published, under the title "A Method of Reaching Extreme Altitudes," a rather thorough mathematical treatment of rocket motion.

And three years later in Germany, Professor Hermann Oberth followed with another mathematical treatise, complete with suggestions for design and construction and with special emphasis on the use of liquid fuels. Oberth was the first man to realize clearly that the change from solid to liquid fuels removed whatever size limit was thus far inherent in solid-fuel rockets. When you switch over to liquid fuels, he stated, there is no theoretical limit to the size of a rocket.

Oberth's book caused the formation of the German Society for Space Travel, the first of the many rocket societies now in existence in many countries. The Society for Space Travel tried to raise the money to actually build liquid-fuel rockets. It finally accomplished this, and at that time, if such a rocket would work at all, it was "success" enough.

But all this merely proved that the liquid-fuel rocket was not inherently impossible. All the real work was still ahead—mountains of work, which needed an army of qualified experts and, it should be added, also mountains of money.

The way history ran in this case, the mountains of money were supplied, reluctantly, by the German Armed Forces. And an army of qualified men was assembled, slowly and under difficulties, by Walter Dornberger, Doctor of Engineering, General of the German Army and head of the Pennemuende rocket station.

But the final proof of the rockets came much later. I was back in med school in my fifth semester at the University of Freiburg when, lying on my bed and my head covered with my pillow as usual, I listened to the 11:00 pm news on BBC: "Today at ten," Malcolm started out earnestly, almost solemnly, "in the morning of November 10, 1944, Prime Minister Winston Churchill finally disclosed in the British Parliament that a

German long-range rocket was in action and that such rockets had fallen in the Greater London area for a number of weeks. Thus he ended a long period of rumors of all kinds."

❖

In 1962, President Dwight D. Eisenhower wrote in his book Crusade in Europe: "It seemed likely that, if the Germans had succeeded in perfecting and using these new weapons six months earlier than they did, our invasion of Europe would have proved exceedingly difficult, perhaps impossible.

I feel sure that if General Dornberger and his men had succeeded in using these weapons over a six-month period, and particularly if he had made the Portsmouth-Southampton area (of England) one of his principal targets, Overlord—code name for the invasion of the European continent in June 1944—might have been written off."

PETER HILGER

FIRST JET FIGHTERS
TAKE TO THE SKY

❦

On August 17, 1944, a month after an attempt to kill *Der Führer,*
(I'll cover this in a later chapter.) there had been an allied air raid
over Germany that stunned the world: during the daylight hours of a
summer afternoon, in clear weather, over 500 B-17s and B-24s flew over
the country to targets in various German cities. But in excess of 150
planes were shot down by the German Luftwaffe that day.

Such losses had never been inflicted during the entire war, nor were
the known Messerschmidt ME 109 fighters capable of bringing down
that many planes. There weren't enough Messerschmidts left anyway.

What happened? asked the world.

What happened? asked the German people, who did not know
whether to be elated or more fearful of increased and intensified air raids
from then on.

What seemed to emerge as a plausible answer at that time was that
this day would be the start and also the end of the life of the first German
jet fighters to see combat, the ME 262. Much later, after the war had
ended, my dentist and a former Luftwaffe pilot who had flown these
planes, verified to me over drilling half of my teeth open (or so it felt) that

84

after the successful August raid on the Allied Air Fleet, the German jet fighters were ordered to land at once at a German Air Base near Munich any time Allied planes entered German air space. These claimed "air bases" consisted mostly of confiscated hay barns directly adjacent to the just finished *Autobahn* between Munich and Augsburg. The lanes of this highway were used as runways for these fighters.

The ME 262's speed was two to three times faster than the speed of the Allied propeller-driven bombers. They could also fly twice the altitude of the prop planes. They howled through the sky, leaving behind long vapor trails and a whining sound, both unfamiliar to the people on the ground. Descending from altitudes unattainable by the American bombers, they passed over Allied formations so fast that the B-24s fell defenseless from the skies like flies.

Never again were they used during the remainder of the war. No one on either side knew officially and for sure the reason of their withdrawal: sabotage on the part of the German officers? A deal Hess may have made in England? Or simply lack of jet fuel?

Much later, after the war, news emerged that Hitler was thought to have ordered the conversion of all ME262 jet fighters into bombers, a process that would have taken many months. Before this order could be completed, the war had ended.

The Allied forces never had an opportunity to see any one of these jets from close up, until one day in April 1945 when a German pilot, on a test flight, suddenly veered west across Allied lines and landed his ME262 in Frankfurt's Rhein Main Airport, by then a United States Air Force Base.

Yet, if these fighters would have continued to fly, they would have significantly altered the outcome of the war during this last year of combat.

But the German people were right when they feared greater intensity of Allied raids. And I was caught right in the middle between the two disputing, fighting sides, as an alien in Germany.

WHEN THINGS GET TOUGH
1944 IN FRANKFURT

⋄

Meanwhile, the war raged on in Europe. Launched by Colonel Count Stauffenberg, of the country's elite division, an assassination attempt on Hitler's life on July 20, 1944, had failed.

Hitler had Stauffenberg executed—without a trial—three days thereafter.

The Gestapo became brutal, tightened the rules, checked out everyone, made house calls, knocked on doors during the night to arrest and deport those who were thought suspicious of attempting to kill *Der Führer* again. Or those who were Jewish or, if Christian, considered the slightest form of a threat to the regime of brutal dictatorship, as was the famous Pastor Bonhöffer and many others who were ultimately killed in Buchenwald.

My situation had deteriorated in many ways. Surely, I wanted to continue my studies at the University of Freiburg, but I also wanted to at least obtain and complete all papers necessary to exit Germany via Switzerland to the United States. Crossing the border to neighboring Switzerland without any permit, I would have been shot dead for sure. German border guards made certain no one would ever leave Hitler's "worker paradise" unauthorized and alive. They were ordered by the

Gestapo to shoot to kill on sight.

Even my father, who had always thought the United States would never enter into a war with Germany because of the many people in the country with German origins like himself, began to see the reason for my efforts to leave. Since I was born and grew up in Europe, I had never been to the United States before, but now that I was of legal age and Germany was in an upheaval and sliding down into defeat, it was time to go, to leave Germany as soon as possible.

The Swiss had taken over the representation of the United States in wartime Germany. I knew their nearest consulate was in Frankfurt. So, during the latter part of October 1944, returning from hospital duty in Heerdt by train to Freiburg for the winter semester at med school, I disembarked at Frankfurt's Central Railroad Terminal, intending to stay for three hours before the next train. The consulate was located downtown three blocks away, an easy walk. There I could obtain and fill out the necessary forms for a Swiss Visa and a U.S. passport for travel to the United States.

Thus far I had always carried Dad's identification papers with me wherever I went, but of course never showed them to the Nazis. For them, I had a bogus German identity card.

The Swiss consul I was directed to greeted me with a typical "Gruetsie," then asked me to sit down. He was polite but non-committal. He handed me the most recent application forms, explained a few necessities for me to watch for and suggested I should go out into the lobby to fill them out, then tell his secretary when I was ready.

An hour later, I had finished and was shown back to his office. But I wasn't quite sure what would be next, what I still had to do, if anything. So I asked him a few additional questions:

"How will all this work? I mean, my return to the United States? I have no car and go to school at the University of Freiburg."

"We will process your application with the American Embassy in Bern," he replied guardedly. "When they issue your passport, we are in agreement with the Americans that we transport you across the Swiss border with our diplomatic couriers. They will stop in Freiburg to pick you up. It's on the way to Basel, so that's easy."

"Then what?"

"We will drive you to Bern, where the American personnel of your Embassy will take over. As far as I can tell you now, they will somehow manage to send you to Lisbon, probably on an U.S. Embassy plane, then book passage for you on a ship to New York. Once there, you will be on your own."

"Fine, that's reassuring. Thank you for helping me out."

Then he passed copies of my completed application back to me. I stuffed them into my duffel. He retained the original, the one that counted.

Without another word, he turned his attention back to his files.

I left the consulate feeling elated and hopeful that it would all happen the way the consul had outlined it. In this turbulent, dangerous wartime, one never knew how things would turn out.

It would NOT turn out that way at all! Much later, in rethinking the entire visit, I often wondered if the stuffy Swiss Consul ever felt it could not turn out the way he had so confidently detailed it. I even wondered if he was still alive.

On the way back to the train station in the heart of Frankfurt, I heard the wailing of sirens—by then a familiar sound that was not always taken seriously, as many times the Allied planes would fly elsewhere. I also knew from experience that the *Luftwaffe*'s warning system was regularly too late. I looked up to the sky, searching, listening. I saw and heard nothing and continued to walk. Then suddenly, I did hear it, the thunder of American B-24s approaching. Then the high-pitched, wheezing sound of bombs descending. This terrifying, screeching, long and whining whistle was all too familiar, its decibels descending the full scale, from the barely audible high tones through the sound's full range to a low point, where it would stop for a moment or two before detonation of heavy explosive and utterly destructive devices in ear-piercing blasts nearby. Extremely nearby.

It brought me down fast. All I could do was crouch behind a two-foot-high wall bordering somebody's brownstone front yard, along the sidewalk. It started to rain bombs. I no longer crouched. I lay flat and as close to the wall as I could, even pressing my side against it, with my face down and the back of my head covered with my hands to shield against the falling debris.

Pure hell had ascended to the earth's surface.

Earsplitting detonations, one after another in rapid sequence, glaring fire, crumbling houses, blinding dust—all engulfed me. Then a huge assortment of debris rained down. Furniture, window frames, broken glass, cobblestones, bricks, pieces of metal and segments of rubber flew through the air and covered me from top to toe. After wiping the dust away from my sore eyes already hurt by the inferno's aftermath, I sensed hot flames shooting up toward the dark sky less than twenty yards from where I was lying near the small wall.

It lasted ten minutes or so. Then it was over. To me, it lasted forever. Yet I was alive! I had survived unhurt, however filthy and bloody from bruises and cuts on my neck, arms and legs.

But the building housing the Swiss Consulate did not survive. It had crumpled into a pile of shattered brick. And somewhere in that brick was my application. It would now be until after the war ended before I could apply for my United States passport.

Suddenly the trauma set in. I was surrounded by ruins! Destruction was everywhere. I saw and heard no living soul, only what sounded like a child in pain, a cry from the rubble near me. To try freeing it from the mountains of debris meant having the right tools. I didn't have them. I couldn't find any around me either.

Rest in peace, child!

Now I had no place to go, no place even to clean myself from the dust and the blood crusts on my body's unprotected parts. I had neither food nor water in my backpack, nor was there any place left standing where I could find something to eat or drink.

I found my way back to the railroad station, no more than two blocks away. But the trip meant climbing over tons of debris, broken glass, ragged steel beams and the remains of those who had not been as lucky as I was to come out of this hellhole alive. I do not remember how long it took. To me it was hours. I did not have a wrist watch anymore. It was lost in the bombing.

The terminal was still standing, although heavily damaged, with its glass dome roof broken into a million pieces. The thirty platforms and sixty tracks were not operative anymore. The trains that were caught in the station by the raid looked like ghosts of another world, their locomotives still hissing with the remainder of steam left in their cylindrical boilers. Then they expired with a single powerful sigh. The world fell eerily quiet around me.

I WAS EXHAUSTED AND, IN MORE THAN ONE WAY, TERRIFIED!

Later that night, trucks were organized to take us out of the city one hundred kilometers away to Würzburg. Before we left, we were fed some minimal food in a bomb shelter under the railroad terminal—watery soup and a crust of dry bread—a meal we consumed at midnight in those freezing cold temperatures of a late October night. Told we would leave instantly, we squeezed ourselves into open trucks at two in the middle of the night and waited, standing up and shivering in the cold, until the convoy left at eight the following morning. We were told by rifle-equipped SA guards that our destination was the railroad station in Würzburg.

It took ten hours to get there. Many roads were blocked or closed, many bridges destroyed, much damage everywhere. We spent the following night at the Würzburg terminal in relatively warm and comfortable conditions. Again, only a little watery food was available.

When the next morning—now the second day after the raid—dawned over the city, the stationmaster announced over the loudspeaker a train leaving for Stuttgart. My direction! I had to be on it.

I barely got on it. I hadn't even hoped for a seat. In those days, you would be glad to ride on trains even if there was room only on the couplings between the coaches. I squeezed into one coach. Trying to also get on, the crowds behind me pushed me forward into the corridor that runs along one entire side of the carriage. On most older-type European trains, it served as the access to the sliding doors that opened into the compartments seating eight. And there I stood, cushioned on three sides by human bodies, not able to move one step. At least, I had the advantage to stand directly at a window that I could pull down when the air got too stale.

Out of Würzburg and across the bridge spanning the Main River, the locomotive began to huff and puff. I knew why: we were climbing up to a higher plateau of the Odenwald halfway down to our destination. Its rolling, gentle hills were now bare of all leaves and barren looking in the bright October sun. Its fields were harvested but not yet plowed.

On that open plateau, we rolled to a screeching halt. Five minutes later, Allied fighter planes descended upon our train from nowhere and began strafing the coaches and the old locomotive with rattling gunfire. Again and again, they circled and came howling back. I knew it was part of the Allied strategy that late in the war, during the winter of 1944, to end it at all cost.

Germany's network of railway transportation was still considered a vital link in war-torn central Europe; therefore, the Allies fiercely attacked them, to paralyze the enemy. Even ancient cities like Dresden and civilian targets were now heavily bombed. Severely criticized in post-war years lasting into the nineties, the Pentagon never explained to the public why it had so heavily bombed that ancient German city and killed thousands in the process.

The reason was quite clear and obvious: after the Battle of the Bulge, Hitler thought he had stopped Patton in his tracks. So he was transferring troops again because he needed more manpower in the East to stop the swiftly advancing Soviets. Dresden became the railroad hub for these transports, and the U.S. Army headquarters in London heard about it. Hence the bombing.

The screaming of people's voices, the numerous fallen bodies wounded beyond recovery, all testified to the absurdity of a war of brothers against brothers, started by a madman from Austria.

There was no place to hide, no place to lie down in a coach where even standing room had been at a premium. There was also no escape from the deadly fire. Before it was over, the woman next to me had been mortally hit and fallen. She was just inches away from my arms and heart. A man on my other side had lost his face. His eyes hung out of their cavities like pears on a tree. His head was a pool of blood. Further towards the door, another man had succumbed to his deadly wounds. His eyes were still open but lifeless, still expressing the fear, the horror. His abdomen was ripped open, his guts protruding from the cavernous interior.

These were my brothers up there in the cockpits and behind the guns. It could have easily been me who got killed. But I remained standing, unhurt.

It turned out to be the second time in as many days that I was terrified beyond belief.

We never made it to Stuttgart. After hours of waiting on the open plains and in fear the raid might be repeated, another train picked us up and brought us through the Neckar Valley to Heidelberg.

Almost four days after the raid, I was back in Freiburg—dirty, dusty, hungry, scraped and bloody—but happy to be alive.

The next day, I saw Fritz at the University. Fall semester had already started and I was late for my classes because of the detour caused by the Frankfurt air raid. My face and arms were still scratched up, my head wound now bandaged, my nose adorned with a huge band aid. So Fritz asked: "What in the world happened to you?"

"Got hit, but not killed."

"Good. They tried to kill Hitler on July 20."

"I know. I heard about it. And the man who dared to do it, the Count von Stauffenberg, was shot to death almost immediately thereafter."

"Yes, that's true. He was a distant cousin of mine."

"Is there anyone who is NOT related to you?" I teased him.

"About fifty million people in this country, that's all. But listen. Things get tougher by the minute. I bet the Gestapo knows where you are. You should come out to Umkirch with me. We can hide you, give you other papers. My mother is good at that."

"Thanks. That's nice of you to say. But I think I'm going to be okay here at school. Nobody here knows my foreign nationality background; I am sure of that."

Fritz tapped my shoulder. "Well, be careful then."

I settled in again and resumed attending classes at med school. It all felt so good: no destruction; no bombs; the medieval city of Freiburg intact and charming; the more regular life, to be back among my friends and peers!

But it was not meant to last long: 1944 would soon come to an end.

Everywhere else in Europe the war had intensified. The Germans were in retreat everywhere. The Soviet Army was advancing to westward in great strides. The western Allies had achieved a strong and permanent foothold in Italy and France after D-day. The conquering of Pacific Islands one by one was costly, time consuming and tragic, with hundreds of lives lost. American casualties were heading for the half-million mark. Washington was determined to bring this worldwide disaster to an end. The Allied bombing of non-industrial targets increased, in the hopes the Germans would capitulate.

The world shuddered. Well-meaning citizens of this country hollered, saddened and agonized by the brutal killings of thousands of Germans by American bombs, not understanding that every passing day brought further losses to America's military forces.

Three weeks later, a flock of B-24s came back during the evening hours of Saturday, November 27, 1944, and targeted the city of Freiburg. The night before, I had gone by train to Hinterzarten up fifty-five kilometers in the Black Forest, with Kurt, a buddy from med school. His parents owned a rustic cottage there and we had planned to stay the weekend and do some serious cross-country skiing.

Coming back to the cottage that late afternoon near dusk, we began to hear heavy detonations further down the mountains to the west. They came in short, abrupt sequences, sounding much like distant, muffled machine gun fire. And with that, we knew Freiburg was hit this time.

"Sounds pretty bad," said Kurt as we sat down on the sundeck, on the cottage's west side, with a bottle of local beer in our hands.

It was. From the deck, we could now see but not hear the detonations of heavy bombs, their rapid flashes shooting into the pale evening sky.

"It is," I replied in horror. "Looks like we are really getting hit this time. See those flashes of fire?"

"Yeah, and I am scared."

"So am I, scared beyond belief."

Then we were silent for a long time as we sat side by side, knowing we were both lucky to be where we were, fifty-five kilometers away, 500 meters higher, and feeling more secure in the comfort of having a friend nearby to share the fright of the unknown unfolding below us in the valley.

Meanwhile, the city of Freiburg burned out of control throughout the night. It was the first air raid on the town. We had always hoped it would be spared, as it contained no industry, no military installations. Its main activities revolved around the more than ten thousand students attempting to get themselves an education.

The ancient city was targeted for reasons similar to those that caused Dresden to be targeted. Possibly it was a transportation hub for troops withdrawn from Italy and the south of France. Therefore, it too became part of the Allies' strategy to end the war at all cost. Hitler was still hollering—madly already—victory of the superior race over the western barbarians. But deep inside, *der Führer* must have known it was over.

Kurt and I returned by train the next morning, a Sunday. We knew it would be bad, had intermittently jumped out of bed during the night before to observe the western sky bright red, testifying to a city crumbling and dying in a rage of fire.

The train stopped five kilometers east of town at the Löwen farm, owned by the family of that name for the last 200 years. (Today it is the site of the elegant Löwen Hotel.) The locomotive slowed down to a stop and hissed one more tired time, then died.

"Everybody off board," shouted the engineer; "this is as far as we go. The tracks are all kaput from here forward into town, blown up, charred in the fire."

We walked the rest. No, we didn't walk. We climbed over tons of debris. As we approached the downtown area we witnessed the degree to which most of the historic city was destroyed. But miraculously and thankfully, the fierce raid left unscratched the *Münster*, the one-spire cathedral built in 1285.

"I'll come with you to your house first before I go home," said Kurt.

I lived in a private home, where I had rented a room. It was owned by an elderly widow. We found the house in ashes, a pile of rubble. And those ashes and rubble held the rest of my belongings.

And that included my most precious possession, the cat whisker crystal radio set I had used as my listening post for so long during those tumultuous war years. My link to the world.

I was homeless again. I owned only what I wore.

"Where is my landlady?" I shuddered, more to myself than to Kurt, at the thought of her still being buried beneath all this rubble. But a few men standing nearby heard it. They came over to me.

"Were you living here?"

"Yes, I was, Obviously, no longer."

"She is okay. She was in her bomb shelter in the basement for more than twenty-four hours, covered by several meters of this stuff," said one of the guys, pointing to the heap of stones and wood.

"Who got her out?"

"We did. But when we did, we found this charred book here. We don't know whose it is? Maybe yours?"

I looked at it. "Yes, it is mine. Thanks a lot." I had tears in my eyes. It was charred and half burned. I could hardly read the cover anymore and its title: *The Buddenbrooks*, by Thomas Mann.

It was the only item saved. All my other stuff, however little I owned, was gone. The fierce raid had cleaned me out of everything. I knew I could buy another radio. They were available at a horrendous price on the black market even during these dark years in wartime Germany. But I deplored most the loss of my books, records and notes from four and a half semesters of medical school. But then, the entire School of Medicine lay in ruins. So the loss did not matter that much any more.

"There won't be school anytime soon," said Kurt.

"No, there won't," I agreed.

❖

As the future turned out, the School of Medicine rebuilding began only in the spring of 1947 and was not completed until late1950.

❖

I was physically and mentally exhausted. Still, I waved to the men, to let them know that I was thankful.

"Come on, let's move out of here, buddy," said Kurt.

"Where to?"

Kurt grabbed my arm. "We'll go now to my room. Let's hope it is still standing."

It was. The house where he rented a room sat up on a hill. It had enjoyed a great view onto the city. It turned out to be not badly damaged; most of its windows were shattered, including those in Kurt's room. We entered his quarters and walked straight to the window overlooking the city.

"Oh, my Lord," exclaimed Kurt. We both stood silently, in awe over what we saw: the centuries-old city in ashes, huge piles of rubble of buildings collapsed or burned beyond recognition, or if not totally collapsed, with their walls still partially standing, their ragged lines pointing to the sky like fingers of a man's hand drowning in a rough sea. The 700-year old cathedral, the Müenster, still stood erect, its single spire pointing high into the sky as if to reach for heaven, to ask "Why do you, Lord, allow such misery, such destruction without any sense?"

I stretched out on the floor in Kurt's room that night, covering myself for scarce warmth with my ski jacket. And there, in the eerie silence of the freezing late November night, with no water or food, we had our eyes fixed on the broken window where dark had fallen over a city that had died.

We waited for the next raid to come.

It never did. Yet I shuddered, trembled. Maybe the events of the day, maybe fright, maybe the near freezing night caused it all. My whole body started to shake, my teeth chattered. I heard Kurt's body shaking as well. Hypothermia was on its way for both of us. That's when Kurt said: "Come up here into my bed. We are both freezing. We can better keep warm if we are closer together."

So, whether I liked it or not, I climbed up and huddled with him under his one blanket. We pressed our backs tightly together to preserve most of the warmth that our bodies generated. Then we both fell instantly into an exhausted sleep.

ROYALS RESCUE ME

❦

Early the next morning, Fritz came by to look for me. He had gone to my house first, found it in ruins so thought I'd be with Kurt. Fritz knew him, as well. He had come through the rubble somehow with his horse Hector pulling his two-wheeled buggy.

"Most of the damage and destruction of the raid was done to the center and the northern part of town," he told us, "and that includes the area where the med school was located and where you lived."

"Then how did you make it up here?" we both asked.

"Well, you know where our castle is at Umkirch. It's ten kilometers west of the city. I had to detour way out north to the village of Emmendingen and come through the foothills to avoid the highest piles of rubble in the city."

"And how did Hector make out on all these hurdles?" Kurt wanted to know.

"Fine. He is a good trooper. But do you have a bucket of water for him?"

"No," said Kurt, "the water lines all seem to be disrupted. Nothing comes out of my faucets."

"Okay then," Fritz replied, stroking Hector's neck, "we will have to wait for our return to his stable then. But listen, you two are coming with me now. I'll take you to Schloss Umkirch. We have room for all of us."

Kurt, 1.90 meters tall, had to sit sideways in the tight rear part of the two-wheeler where normally luggage would be stored. That space was empty because we no longer owned any clothing to take along. I shared the bench with Fritz. I do not remember how long it took to get out to the castle, but it probably was quite a long time, probably most of the day. When we finally arrived in the village we guided Hector up to the iron gate adorned with the golden crown of the Hohenzollern family. Once into the carriage-park, Hector stopped on the circular driveway at the mansion's front portal. I hopped down onto the gravel just as the door opened and a charming lady said: "Hallo."

Fritz called out at once: "Mother, these are my friends from school, Gerd and Kurt. Gerd's landlady's house in town was completely destroyed and Kurt's was badly damaged, so I invited them to stay with us."

"Well, of course. Welcome to our small abode, boys. Come on in. Heavens, you must have gone through hell. You are all dusty, torn up and bloody. I will at once talk to Frau Möller to draw a hot bath for you two. And Fritz, you take them up to your room to see if you have the right things for them to wear, you hear?

"Yes, Mother."

Then I walked up to her and said: "Thank you, Royal Highness, for your kindness to take us in."

She extended her right hand face down which I immediately understood as a gesture that indicated she expected me to kiss her hand, as was customary in those days when a man met a lady. Knowing the proper procedure, I placed my left hand on my back, moved forward one step with my right foot, bent down twenty degrees and extended my right hand to reach hers, which was pointing at me inside down. Then my face stopped shortly before my lips closed in on her hand. My dad had taught me the proper etiquette years before: "Never touch the back of her hand with your lips," I heard him say, "unless you are in love with her. Then kiss her hand the way you would place a kiss on her lips. And even then, never do a hand-kiss when the lady wears gloves."

So this was the daughter of the last King of Saxony, a former Princess of Sachsen and now the *Fürstin* Margarete von Hohenzollern. Before breakfast the next morning, she asked me to skip the hand-kiss and call her *Fürstin*. I did not yet know then how she would turn out to be for me such a saint.

That day became the beginning of, altogether, four years living under the protection and shelter of the Hohenzollerns.

Fritz had also taken in a few of his cousins who were enrolled at the University. That morning, I met others staying at Umkirch, also bombed out as I was. They were the three brothers, Dedo, Gero and Timo, all of them Princes von Sachsen; then Georg Duke von Mecklenburg; Konstantin Prince von Bayern; and Count Max Willibald von Waldburg-Wolfegg. Then there was Fritz's younger brother Prince Franz.

No doubt Fritz was our *primus inter pares,* Latin for "first among equals." With one exception, we all adhered to the silent, unwritten rule to follow his final decisions on matters of mutual concern. At 1.74 meters, he was a bit shorter than I—about half a head shorter—but less bulky, more slender. His shock of light blond hair was combed mostly back with a straight-as-a-ruler part line running along the center of his scalp.

Konstantin von Bayern was the tallest of us. He was flamboyant and looked extremely royal. As a grandson of the famous King Ludwig of Bavaria, he had to endure a lot of teasing because of the numerous sugar-baker castles his famous forbear built: the likes of Hohenschwangau and Neuschwanstein, which today can mostly be seen on posters advertising travel to Germany. I did not participate in this sport of joshing him. As the only non-aristocrat in the group, I felt it was not my calling to do so.

The Sachsen princes were medium built, possessed medium intellect, were medium sociable, medium conversing. They were easy-going, fun-loving fellows and therefore just good, faithful friends.

So was brother Franz von Hohenzollern.

Then there was Albert Joshua Burger. He was the son of a Jewish family the *Fürstin* knew. Perhaps as a result of that fact, he never followed any rule made by anyone except the *Fürstin*. He did not even acknowledge Fritz as our *primus inter pares*. As Fritz naturally did occupy his suite alone, Albert was the only other one in the group who had a single room. This arrangement occurred not because we recognized his self-proclaimed "special status" but because he never washed.

I shared a room with Max, so that didn't bother the two of us much. Next to Fritz, he was my favorite. We were the only ones, apart from Fritz, to have a small bathroom attached, with no shower, just one of those mammoth European bathtubs.

Max was very muscular, immensely strong, with a sizable frame but was, as many very strong people often are, very gentle and good-natured. When we had a wasp or mosquito in our room, he'd spend many minutes to catch it alive, then open the window to free the fortunate insect by letting it fly out. Then he would happily grin and go about his daily chores.

He and I became good pals. We also turned into some sort of laughing stock among the group because—even on cold days—every day we soaped then rinsed ourselves standing up in the bathtub's ice-cold water. Sit down in it we did only in the summer. That would've called for just too much bravery during the cold winter days in an unheated bathroom.

All ten of us were between twenty and twenty-two years of age.

Kurt left a week after his arrival to return to his parents' cabin up in

Hinterzarten near Titisee. I took Hector and the two-wheeled buggy to bring him to the western edge of town. From there he had to find his way through the rubble to the Löwen farm, where his eastbound train would leave. On the way home, I started to talk to Hector and rattled off all my anger about this senseless destruction of ancient cities and, above all, human lives. To me, it seemed that Hector nodded. Whatever he appeared to do, it was the beginning of an unusual friendship with a horse!

Yet another close friendship—with Fritz von Hohenzollern—had begun to unfold. It was a human friendship which lasted to this day of writing: more than six decades!

On the second morning after I arrived, Fritz said after breakfast: "I see you are still in your ripped shirt and stained pants. And I apologize for the fact that I forgot you lost everything you owned. Let's go up to my room to see if I have anything that might fit you."

We walked upstairs and looked at each other in a measuring way for the first time. That turned out to be so funny that we both burst out laughing: "Looks like I am sizing you up like I would a pretty girl. It's not that way. Just wanted to see if I have roughly the same body lines you do," I told him.

"Oh, I know that's what you had in mind. That's what I too had in mind when I sized you up."

In his bedroom, he opened his closets. There were three of them, each large, with two shelves above the coat hanger racks. All three were packed with clothes, a great variety of them, for all and every occasion, it seemed. He was better endowed with clothes than I ever was. And my mom had not been skimpy in outfitting her kids. But now, all I owned, I wore. Shabby, torn and dirty.

"Look, here is a Loden coat I haven't worn for a while. It's old, has some bloodstains on it, I believe; yeah, here they are. They came from the many hunting trips it survived. Try that on."

I did. It fit to a T. I took it off and wanted to hang it up again when Fritz said: "It's yours."

We spent well over an hour up there, looking for what could fit me. Ultimately, I came down with two pair of corduroy pants that were wider cut than others and just about fit me. I also inherited two of his footwear outfits, one a pair of dress shoes, the other hiking boots. But for the rest of the clothing I needed, our sizes were too different. His shirts were all too tight for me, because my chest was wider. His socks and sweaters were too tight, as well.

"Thanks for all this. I don't know what I could have done without it."

"Ah. But we are not done yet. Now we will go to Maria. She is from the Ukraine. Her German is not that good but she has a heart of gold."

She was the seamstress. She had her domain in the tower where most of the servants slept. "I rarely come here," he told me when we climbed the circular stairs. "So it's about time I check things out again."

When Fritz entered, she got out of her chair and fell down on one knee, crossed, then folded her hands under her chin as if to pray. Fritz lifted her up and said: "Maria, please stand up. This is my friend. He is staying with us now. He lost everything he owned. I found some clothes for him in my closets, but our sizes are different for feet, legs, chests and height. Can you make him the rest, like shirts, sweaters, socks, handkerchiefs, gloves?"

Maria's height reached only to where my heart is. She was also missing a lot of teeth. But what she missed in height and teeth, she more than made up in smiles and friendliness.

"I can make shirts, hankies very well, from big strong linen. Not others, Highness. Johanna will do. She knitting, from sheep's wool."

"Okay, then get Johanna to talk to my friend here, and you and she get together and take his measurements."

"Ja, Your Highness."

Maria made five shirts for me, three with long sleeves and two with short ones. They were the kind her men wore in the Ukraine, without a collar, just a bordered edge at the top. They were cut wide at the shoulders and on down the arms to the elbows, then skintight to the wrists. Kozak shirts, I called them. The famous Russian dancers by that name always wore them. That was the only design Maria knew. They were made out of a very heavy, very durable linen, the kind we make work cloth out of in this country. They lasted forever!

Johanna was old already. She'd been with the Hohenzollerns for almost fifty years. She did not work anymore but now lived out her retirement years where she spent practically her entire adult life, in Umkirch. Now she knitted. For me, she knitted for more than four weeks. By the time January arrived, I had a huge stack of woolen socks, several pairs of mittens and two long-sleeve sweaters. I was ready for the winter outdoors. I had to take all her knittings up to her room and wear them for her to see and approve. She beamed with happiness and pride.

❖

I still have one pair of the mittens and two pairs of socks. The Kozak shirts I wore for years, then placed them in drawers for some future camping trips. One of them went with me on my motorcycle safari to Alaska in 1987.

❖

Schloss Umkirch, my new home, was a wonderful place, not fancy, not rich with baroque signatures, but simple, and in its simplicity extremely elegant. In many ways it reminded me of my childhood when I spent summer vacations at Landfort, my mother's ancestral home in Holland. Both were about the same size; both were laid out pretty much alike.

The mansion in Umkirch was built during the early 1800s by King Carol I of Romania, a born Prince von Hohenzollern, who used it as a summer home in his native Germany. The king, a great-uncle of Fritz's father Friedrich Wilhelm *Fürst* von Hohenzollern, willed it to him upon his death. He and Fritz's mother, the former Margarete Princess von Sachsen and daughter of the last King of Saxony, lived there for many years. But when Friedrich Wilhelm senior died and Friedrich Wilhelm junior became the *Fürst*, they moved back into the Sigmaringen Burg. The *Fürstin*, however, preferred Umkirch and divided her time between both places. Fritz and his six siblings grew up there.

After the terror of the preceding months, Umkirch was heaven to me. All of us youngsters slept in the east wing upstairs. Fritz had a suite: his bedroom with bath attached was connected to a living room that would henceforth be the place where all of us hung out. Franz had his own room too. The rest of us doubled up in a row of guest rooms, which were separated by a bathroom in their center and accessible by both sides.

Fritz's parents, the *Fürst* and *Fürstin*, occupied the upstairs west wing when they were in residence.

Downstairs, to the east of the sizable foyer, was a salon used for receptions, a living- or sitting-room as Fritz's mother called it, a music room and a winter garden filled with exotic plants and trees. To the west was a dining room with seating for sixty-four and a smaller one for twelve, which we used, then a pantry and substitute kitchen where the food brought up from the kitchen house was prepared for serving. Behind it were storage rooms and other utilities.

Max's and my bedroom upstairs was almost over the front portal, which opened to a wide, circular gravel driveway. The portal itself was shaded by a large portico, its two-story height supported by the traditional four gothic columns. Cars and carriages could pass through it to embark or disembark passengers while simultaneously shielding them from sun and rain.

Our magnificent view swept across a well-cut meadow that appeared endless and lost itself in the distance among the park's century old oaks and evergreen Lerche pines. Yonder were the gentle hills of the Kaiserstuhl, and the Rhine River, still young and much narrower than it was 550 miles farther north, where it empties into the North Sea at Rotterdam.

After the air raid, Freiburg's university was closed until further notice. The entire med school lay in ashes. The university would not reopen until the start of the winter semester 1945/46 and even then, the med school remained closed. Its pile of rubble hadn't even been touched yet. There was no money for that.

Nor was there money for much else. Food was extremely scarce and tightly rationed. The Black Market blossomed.

But I was safe now. December moved onto the calendar. It got colder. Snow started to fall. But we had plenty of wood from the royal forests to keep us warm. I had a bed, things to wear and, above all, my friends around me. I grew a beard. I also changed my name. The *Fürstin* had suggested then arranged it. I was now called Schultheiss, Peter Schultheiss, in accordance with my new official identity. And on one of her visits to Berlin, she even arranged—with someone whose name she never mentioned—for a German passport in the name of Peter Schultheiss. She handed it to me with a devilish smile on her face.

From then on, I showed it to the Gestapo when they came by to check on all of us and our doings, which happened often but irregularly. When they talked to me, I was scared to death that they might find out that my passport was bogus.

The *Fürstin* also kept us and the rest of the numerous Hohenzollern family safe by maintaining a liaison with the Nazi leaders in Berlin. She did not do so because she believed in their cause. But the Hitler regime strongly disliked aristocrats and the *Fürstin* thought it advantageous to be on good terms with the regime by being on good terms with Adolf Hitler. She knew Hitler appreciated charming women. And that she definitely was.

But Hitler had his own agenda as well. He needed a high-level contact among the aristocracy to keep his officers of the Army pacified. Through centuries of tradition, the majority of military officers came from the aristocracy, even those in Hitler's armed forces.

So we were safe from the Gestapo. When their Mercedes Compressor rolled to the front portal on the gravel driveway, they never asked the Hohenzollerns for their identity papers, likely under direct orders from Hitler himself. But the Gestapo knew I was not part of the family, so when they asked me for my papers, I had them. I never aroused their suspicion because I spoke their language fluently. What they never knew was that when they came, my heart rate went up way over one hundred beats.

I was scared beyond belief!

The *Fürstin* told us later, after the war had ended, that every time she was invited by *der Führer* to a state dinner in Berlin, he would choose her as his "Tischdame" sitting on his right. She explained to us that the man had an often supernatural power over many women. She described it as almost spellbinding, that he was a hypnotizer, perhaps. Over her as well? I thought definitely not, knowing her disgust with his brutal regime.

❖

Sixty years later, in 2006, a writer by the name of Paul Hollander explained it well in his book The End Of Commitment, which S. T. Karnick, an associate fellow of the Indianapolis-based Sagamore Institute, reviewed in part:

"Hollander astutely observes," Karnick writes, "in a discussion of Soviet dissident and literary scholar Lev Kopelev, that his and others' faith in socialism was really a substitute religion, a matter of profoundly and genuinely religious attitudes and beliefs.' "Kopelev's struggles," he notes, "indicate that intellectuals—no less than ordinary people, possibly more so—long for sustaining beliefs." Hollander writes vividly of Soviet intellectuals who endured frequent collisions with the authorities and even more persistent shock and revulsion at the brutality the Communist leadership engaged in and required their underlings to carry out.

"During World War II in eastern Germany, for example, unlike most of his fellow countrymen in the army, [Kopelev] was revolted by the raping of women, the casual killing of civilians, the looting and wanton destruction of properties." As a result of his attempts to prevent these atrocities, he was accused of undermining morale and eventually was arrested and given a harsh sentence by the Stalin Regime, known for brutality.

Languishing in prison, Kopelev nonetheless tried to convince his fellow inmates that the problem with the Soviet Union was Stalin, not Communism. Through all this and more, Hollander observes, Kopelev desperately attempted "to cling to ideas and ideals that he himself realized were deeply flawed and crumbling. For disillusioned individuals living under Communist regimes, there were only two real alternatives: staying and serving the system they had come to regard as unacceptably corrupt, or leaving for the West. To stay and try to fight the system would be certain death."

Yes, Paul Hollander, you are so right in that assumption!

❖

During this late period of WWII and a time when there was total blackout of any foreign news in Nazi Germany, we regularly hung around the elaborate shortwave radio system the *Fürst* and *Fürstin* had hidden in an underground tunnel that led to the farmhouses. The antennas were stored in the farthest attic corner of the mansion, well covered by the spider webs and dust that had accumulated over the centuries. A long cable hidden behind wallpapered walls connected them to the radio located in a small, moist, mildew-laden alcove of the tunnel where our megaphone to the world was installed.

I rejoiced at seeing and using another cat whisker. After losing my own at the air raid on Freiburg, it was like *deja vu* for me.

I taught those who didn't know the device how to operate it, where the BBC was on the stone. Yet most of us knew already how to bring it into the earphones.

Late in the evening, we would tiptoe into the damp tunnel, then crawl to the radio to listen to BBC give us the latest on the status of the war. We thought the British maintained this special newscast spoken in German by a Brit who was dubbed Lord Haw-Haw. But he soon turned out to be Lord Haw Haw, aka William Joyce, the British traitor. When we heard him first, we thought him to be the real BBC, but we soon detected hidden resemblances to Hitler's huge propaganda machine orchestrated by Goebbels. We ultimately found the REAL BBC and their reliable broadcaster Malcolm. He spoke the real English. I could tell.

Such activity was strictly forbidden in Hitler's Germany. If anyone had betrayed us to the Gestapo *(Geheime Staatspolizei)*, we would be accused of *Landesverat* (treason), and hanged that same day. The SS was omnipresent. They were everywhere and in civilian clothes as well. So we made sure that some of us would not be involved—like Albert, whom we didn't trust, or Franz, Fritz's younger brother then only sixteen years old, who would have had the capacity to involuntarily blabber out to others what we were doing so late at night.

We were exceptionally dependent on the short wave connection to the world during and after the Yalta conference. We soaked up any detail we could muster to guide us into our immediate, and hopefully peaceful, future.

"I listened to the BBC last night when Malcolm pointed out that Marshall Montgomery consistently submitted his plan to advance further east than the Elbe River to Berlin," I volunteered one evening upon returning from the tunnel after midnight. "But apparently the Supreme Commander General Eisenhower turned him down each time because he stuck to the Yalta Agreement and his respect for the Soviet Union's Marshal Georgi Zhukov."

❖

Perhaps had Eisenhower known at that point that a few years later the Cold War would accelerate beyond all expectations, he might have agreed with Marshall Montgomery and General Patton. It might have avoided the Berlin Blockade from June 24, 1948, to September 30, 1949, and ultimately the Wall in 1960, which for thirty long years stood as a divider of not only Germany but the entire world.

❖

"I hear Roosevelt is really sick now. Crippled badly, I guess, by his polio," said Konstantin von Bayern in a low voice, more or less to himself.

"I wonder who will occupy us? I bet—and hope—it will be the U.S. Army," I whispered one night.

"Better be the French," Fritz shouted before we could hush him. He then continued with a low voice: "We are related to the French royal family and most of their generals are also related to us. They will treat us better than the cowboys from the far away prairies."

"I think it should be the British. They are gentlemen. I know. My mother is from Britain. They wouldn't hurt us," Georg von Mecklenburg added in hardly audible tones.

And so we theorized, we hoped, we silently prayed for the end— whatever it may be—to come soon.

After the war ended, I never thought of our great British service again and where it came from in Umkirch. And during the last sixty years I always forgot to ask Fritz whether the equipment still existed in the attic and tunnel. I am willing to bet even he forgot. And I am also sure it's all still where it used to be, rotten and rusted now, to be found one day by another generation who will marvel at these pieces of rusted metal and exclaim:

"What in the world did they use THAT for?"

At Umkirch, we had enough to eat. Not fancy stuff, just basics. The 965-acre farm took care of that, with livestock, timber and hay its main sources of revenue. The eighteen small farmhouses were mostly occupied by farm workers and their families. Many of them were second-, third- or even more generation workers for the Hohenzollerns. The main farmhouse, inhabited by the farm manager, was attached to the stables and barns on one side.

Further attacks on nearby Freiburg did not happen.

Except for Fritz, everyone helped out on the farm. Fritz was naturally most involved with managing the whole operation in Umkirch. The *Furst* and *Furstin* lived further east near the large Hohenzollern Burg at Sigmaringen.

I was put in charge of practically everything with wheels; my foremost task was to take care of and operate the Fahr tractor. I named him Max. Because he was as strong as an ox. Tractor Max and I plowed the fields, cut the hay, or pulled the felled trees out of the royal forests surrounding us.

When we began work in the morning, I had to get up half an hour earlier and start the wood fire in the tractor so that we had enough pressure to produce the gas it needed to run. Never an early riser, I had to admit it was hard at first. But once I got the hang of the start-up procedure, I could roll around in bed a bit longer.

Start the wood fire? What did I mean by that? The job was more difficult than it sounds: we didn't have enough fuel to operate the beast, so it was converted to wood gas. That meant an oven-like, cylindrical structure mounted on the vehicle's rear between the two large wheels. It was fired with wood chips. A small compressor helped to stoke the fire to a high degree of heat in an otherwise closed, air-tight container. The escaping gas was channeled into the engine in lieu of gasoline.

The tractor's output of horsepower was about one-third of what it would produce if powered by fossil fuel. The only truck on the farm, of which I was also the driver, produced a remarkable rate of one-half of normal when stoked up. It was lighter by at least 1,000 pounds.

My buddy Max was stocky and very muscular. His strength was immense. That's why I named the tractor after him. I always relied on Max, my friend and roommate, when I used Max the tractor to haul whole trees from the woods back to the farm. They were then cut up into firewood for the numerous tiled space stoves in the mansion and farmhouses.

He could always lift the logs high enough so that I could slide a chain underneath the tree trunk. As Max did that, the veins in his bull's neck popped out big and blue. He never blinked an eye. To him it was all fun. But if ever anyone had attacked me, Max would have risen to the occasion. People backed away because they saw his strength unfold. Even the Gestapo guys visiting occasionally to check out everyone kept their safe distance from him.

Only when the French troops came and made all of us lie on the driveway's harsh surface could Max not do anything because he was a prisoner as well, stretched out flat on the gravel with a gun barrel on his neck and a French soldier's boot on his back.

I loved my tractor Max. It was in my charge for well over a year. It was slow, huge and clumsy. But it always worked. And its oily smell, so familiar to me over time, made him my friend too. Once in a while, way out in the fields, I had to get out of my contoured steel saddle, jump down to the ground and re-stoke the fire. Then I would have to wait a while until the gas pressure was up again. Yet one has to do likewise enjoying a wintry evening by a fireplace. A happy task!

Then there was the large lorry with a tongue for a two-horse hitch, or three, even four. We used it rarely. It carried up to six persons sitting up front on two benches and provided a large loading area in the back for hay, supplies, oats, leaves and whatever else needed to be carried from one place to another on the farm.

We no longer had two horses to pull it. Hector was the only one left. All others had been drafted by the Wehrmacht. So we let Hector pull it alone by hitching him onto one side of the center tongue, which limited the weight of the loads we could haul.

Then there was the-two wheeled buggy with two parallel tongues between which Hector was harnessed. It was the one Fritz used to haul Kurt and me from the destroyed city of Freiburg. It was really the only mode of transportation we had. But it was limited in room for only two people comfortably or three uncomfortably on its narrow bench, unless a person small and slender came along who could squeeze into the minute space behind the bench. Franz usually rode there; he fit the physical measurements of the space.

My duties included maintaining these two essential carriers to whatever extent I could, considering the extreme scarcity of everything to repair them when the necessity arose.

The sizeable garage not far from the circular entrance to the castle held the three royal vehicles of the family. The largest was a 1938 Maybach chauffeur-driven limousine with seating for eight and a twelve-cylinder power plant under the hood, which made the engine compartment look as long as the coach section behind it. It stood so high you could step into it upright. It was a monstrous vehicle. Another was a sleek Mercedes sports coupe Compressor with the longest hood I had ever seen. Huge, flexible metal pipes mounted on the side of the hood fed the air needed for the additional pressure into the carburetors. These cars were clocked at 180 km (112 mph), an unheard of speed for motor vehicles in those days. Hitler was driven in one like it. The third was a non-descript Audi used primarily by the staff. All of them, inactive for lack of fuel, were covered by sheets.

I did not have to worry about them as part of my responsibilities. Even after the war was over, we could not drive any of them until late in 1947.

Even then, their use was limited due to lack of spare parts and the huge amount of gasoline they consumed.

And then, of course, there was my friend Hector. Although the animals on the farm—cows, hogs, chicken, sheep, geese and goats—were tended by our French prisoner farm hands, Hector became my responsibility because he was part of our rolling stock. But the real reason was undoubtedly that the French prisoners were deadly afraid of this huge animal. They had routinely neglected his care until I came to his rescue in November 1944.

When I saw him for the first time in the otherwise empty horse barn, he stamped his right hoof. He snorted, as horses tend to blow air through their nostrils when they are nervous. His eyes flared with the wildness often displayed by stallions. When I approached his gate, I began whispering to him. This went on for some twenty to thirty minutes until he finally decided to come closer. In another hour, he had edged to the gate. When I then ever so slowly stretched out my hand through the iron bars and began to run my fingers down his right cheek and his long, wide nose, he held still. His eyelids then started to droop a bit and he looked peaceful. I knew I was close to having Hector on my side. Only once more did he scream out in retreat, seemingly as mad as he always had been to the others. But then, a short while later, he came back to me.

Fritz, who had happened into the stable to look for me, was aghast when he saw me stroke Hector's neck. He hollered: "Don't go close to him. He is not used to you."

"Yes, he is. He is just checking me out."

"But he is dangerous. He'll make mincemeat out of you. Come on back, please," he shouted.

"Don't worry, I will make friends with him," I said.

Hector had looked up when Fritz spoke but was now stretching his nostrils through the iron gate bars for me to touch them. And although

I had no previous experience with horses, I knew from breeding and training hunting dogs that this was a sign of trust. So I opened the gate very softly and let the approaching animal sniff me over and check me out.

We linked up. Then I knew we had bonded.

Hector was big and exceptionally strong. I was six feet tall but could not see over his rump when I brushed him or hosed him off. The color of his short coat was a caramel brown, and his light-brown mane and tail were long. He might have been a Belgian horse, of the same breed as those Clydesdales Anheuser Busch still uses now to pull the ceremonial beer wagons.

From then on, I was the only one who could walk into his stable.

From then on, he would often stamp his right hoof again when I entered his space because he had heard my footsteps and he knew it was me. I would call out HEW – HEW then and he would come up, rub his cheek on my shirt and push his soft lips to my pockets to see if I brought his favorites: sugar cubes or carrot sticks. If I had them—which would be most of the time—I would place those goodies on my right hand stretched out flat so he could nip them with his lips without using his teeth.

From then on, I was the one who tended to him, fed him, cleaned him, hosed him down, rubbed him dry and later brushed his short-haired rump. When I used the brush on his belly I had to crawl under him; he would let out small sighs of sheer pleasure. He would never move. And when I was finished, he would invariably sling his huge head over my right or left shoulder so that his cheek would press on mine. And then I always held still.

In spite of his macho behavior toward others, Hector seemed amazingly human and never faltered in his trust of me. When I left Umkirch in the fall of 1947 to move back to Freiburg, I spent considerable time in the horse barn to say good-bye to my four-legged friend.

❖

Fritz told me in Vancouver in 1955 that with a decreased load of work, Hector had lived on for two more years, then was put out to pasture in retirement. He expired one night in the same horse barn I knew. Fritz had him buried in the castle's extensive park grounds.

Looking at Hector from the perspective of today, some sixty years later, he would have been an ideal candidate for the Robert Redford movie The Horse Whisperer.

❖

Frau Josefine Möller and her crew of domestic help took care of our nourishment and well-being. The farm employed two foremen and a large number of French prisoners of war who'd rather work with us than be cooped up in camp. Besides, they were also given enough to eat and were treated just as farmhands.

The kitchen and supply rooms were housed in a separate building about thirty yards away, tucked in behind shrubbery and shaded by century-old oak trees. Frau Moller reigned over those areas too.

Every three months a Schlachtfest happened, a major slaughter operation requiring the work of practically all servants and farmhands. The ten of us were exempt. I was extremely glad for that because wading in animal's blood was not ever a chore I enjoyed. A row of hogs—their number depending on how many people were to be fed—was slaughtered that day, then processed by hand: roasts, kidneys, ham, liver, skin. Nothing was thrown away. Even the intestines were used, to be stuffed with a concoction made of the hog's blood. It was called *Blutwurst* or blood sausage: fresh blood still warm from the animal was mixed with large chunks of lard from the layers between the skin and muscles, than heavily seasoned and broiled to a stuffing to fill the Wurst.

Fritz explained: "On Schlachtfest days, we eat only soup. Everyone is involved with the slaughter operation. There's no help in the kitchen."

I never quite understood that rule because the cook and her helper never participated in the slaughter.

But the day following the Schlachtfest, every one of us ten youngsters, the servants, farm hands and including every single French prisoner helping in the fields—all of us were served the same huge dinner: a dish called *Himmel und Erde,* meaning sky and earth. It was cooked of apple sauce, growing near the sky, and potatoes harvested from below the ground. With it came generous portions of the fresh *Blutwurst* made the day before, roasted in large pans and minced with a heap of lard and onions grilled to a crisp brown. It definitely made the wurst more tolerable. Besides, when you are hungry, everything tastes good. And although we had enough to eat, we were always hungry, a phenomenon natural to young guys working outdoors all day.

It tasted marvelous, was probably loaded with cholesterol-adding ingredients and gave us a lot of new energy. Later, after the war had ended, I shuddered at the thought of eating it again and always tried to politely decline.

But all ten of us got along fine and spent much of our free time together hunting deer to augment our food supply. Later, during the evenings, we would listen to jazz on the radio's American Forces Network station, first on shortwave, then, when the American Army occupied southern Germany, directly from its studio in Munich. That, of course, also supplied us with the latest news on how the war was proceeding.

During that winter, Fritz's dark-brown German shorthair pointer bitch Alfa had a litter of five, fathered by his male pointer Rex, who was speckled white-brown.

"Pick a pup. Raise him. Train him or her. If you've never done that, I'll teach you how," Fritz told me.

I picked a dark-brown female and named her Adda.

We always had enough food scraps for all the dogs in Umkirch's extensive kennels. Many of them were hunting dogs, all of those owned by any one of us ten. During that winter and spring of 1945, with the help and knowledge of Fritz, I raised and trained Adda to be a hunting dog. Later that spring, I would—as I always did—take all the dogs out to the field with me when I worked the tractor. But now that I had Adda—who, incidentally, slept on an old blanket at the foot of my bed every night, just like Max's male pointer did at the foot of his—she got to ride ON the tractor with me during the day.

I also remember a trip in January 1945 to another village about twenty-one kilometers away in the Kaiserstuhl, an area of hills between the Rhine to the west and Freiburg to the east. A family by the last name of Henkel, whom my parents had known well when they all lived in Düsseldorf in peacetime, maintained a vineyard out there in the rolling countryside. It included an old farmhouse converted to more modern status. I went there with the two-wheeler drawn by Hector at Christmas 1944 and had planned to take Fritz along to introduce him to the next generation owners, son Konrad and daughter Lisa. The latter was married to a Dr. Pettersen.

Fritz and I loaded the small two-wheeler with excess farm tools to barter for wine at their place. But at the last minute, another urgent matter prevented Fritz from going with me. So I went alone.

I then found out they badly needed not farm tools but farm food, and I knew we needed the new crop of wine, to drink but foremost to barter for farm equipment to run our lifeline. Already, Konrad and Lisa had inherited and ran the family enterprise, a large plant producing household items like cleaning agents, soap etc. (In the late eighties, they bought Clorox in the U.S.)

On the way back, a horde of wild boars crossed the road in front of me, about ten animals. I retrieved my hunting rifle from the back seat, slowed my buggy to a stop, aimed at the herd—using the space between Hector's ears as my focus—and fired one single shot. A large boar fell, but I fell as well, hard, back on the wooden bench of my buggy. Because Hector took off like a bullet. I got him under control before we were home. But later that afternoon, I told Fritz of the incident: "I shot a wild boar."

"You did what?"

"Yeah, across Hector's ears. I almost lost him too."

"Where is the animal?"

"Where I killed it."

"Let's get it now, before others find it. Boars are excellent meat. Frau Möller will be happy."

That early evening, when dark was just setting in, we left again with Franz to retrieve the boar. It was indeed too valuable to leave out in the fields unguarded. Smoked boar ham tastes especially good!

On February 4, 1945, the three major Allies at war with Hitler held their summit conference in Yalta, on the Soviet Union's Crimean Peninsula in the northern Black Sea. Churchill came from England, Stalin rode the train down from Moscow and—two months before his death—a feeble and dying Roosevelt represented the United States.

❖

Due to his progressing physical infirmity, the American President was later reported to have failed to fully comprehend what was transpiring at the conference. He was blamed by some historians and politicians for granting too many concessions to a confident Stalin, concessions which would later haunt the western Allies.

❖

Much of the city of Yalta had been raided and destroyed by the German occupation forces. The once luxuriously furnished hotels for the Russian aristocracy were dilapidated and had been robbed of any furniture and utensils. The Soviet government had to scramble to ship loads of everything by train from Moscow hotels, everything the western Allies would consider normal in their respective countries. The conference was held to determine three major issues:

- How to achieve a peaceful encounter of all armies in the center of Germany;

- How to construct a postwar Germany;

- How to handle the France and China situations.

The French were not invited, a fact which General de Gaulle would never forget nor forgive the Allies for. The agreement of Yalta determined that their future occupation zone would be created out of territories conquered by the United States and Britain. Neither did they participate in the post-war Potsdam conference to determine the fate of Berlin.

Later in February of 1945, I took another journey to Lisa Henkel Pettersen's vineyard. This time it turned out to be a horror trip. Again I used Hector and the same buggy and went for the same purpose of bartering. But this time Fritz came along.

"Lisa, Doctor, this is my friend, the Erbprinz von Hohenzollern. We came to bring you the tools you need, and a pair of pruning shears for your vineyards."

"Thank you so much. We are really in bad need of the items. Now come in and plan to stay for supper," Lisa said with that brilliant smile of hers.

I loved that smile. The Henkels made—among many other products—a well-known cleaning powder called Persil. I was sure Lisa used it on her teeth!

And supper automatically came with—you guessed it—wine: their own, of course, several varieties.

We left at ten. The moon was out full. It was a brilliant night.

"Don't forget the cases of wine. The servants placed it near your buggy," Lisa called out to us as we approached the small two-wheeler. We had tied up Hector at a tree. He was standing there dozing.

"Thanks, we found it."

Fritz plunked down on the right side of the narrow bench and said: "Wow, why am I so sleepy?"

"It's all that wine."

"Can't be. I don't recall more than one glass."

"Go to sleep, buddy," I grinned back. "You're not missing a thing. I could go to sleep too because Hector knows the way home by now."

Fritz was out of it before I could load the cases of wine.

I took the reins. Now, driving a buggy back in the moonlight, with a horse pulling it that could gallop home fully asleep because it knows the way so well, is admittedly less dangerous than driving an automobile under those conditions.

But what no one ever told me is what I should do if I encountered a tank. Yes, there it was, a German Tiger tank, a massive monster without lights, its huge gun pointed straight at me. The moon was out, providing sufficient light, but my mind was so foggy it took me a while to realize what I was facing. This time, my temperamental companion Hector did not rise or attempt to gallop away. He probably knew better. He must have realized there was no gain in bucking a German Army tank. So my Hector volunteered to stop on his own. Good for him. His horse sense was a lot better than mine.

The Wehrmacht lieutenant in the turret called out for me to pull aside, which I obediently did. I even managed to say *danke* when the monster rattled by.

Fritz slept through it all.

GENERAL PATTON'S ADVANCE TO THE RHINE AND BEYOND

⚜

By early March 1945, British troops had advanced through the center of The Netherlands into the northern half of Germany, their future area of occupation. Patton had fought the bloody, fierce Battle of the Bulge during the preceding winter months. "The Bulge? What do they mean by that?" we wondered.

Malcolm explained it that evening over the shortwave from London as we listened in the dark and moist, mildew-filled tunnel: "Picture the map of Europe. For months, yes, even years now, we have shown you where we stood and where the Germans had lined up to defend the European continent. Allied invasions caused little dents in those lines by Patton invading Sicily, by the invasion of June 6, 1944, into Normandy, by Stalin pushing the Germans back west from Moscow and Stalingrad. By the winter 44/45, these lines had been moved much closer to the German heartland.

"Then came Hitler's winter attack in southern Belgium. The map suddenly showed an increasingly deeper bulge to the west, again between Aachen and Luxembourg, even as far as Bastingnon in France. That's where the Germans succeeded to cut off the Americans. Hitler's Army took no prisoners. GIs died by the thousands."

I shuddered at the thought when I heard it in the tunnel and rushed upstairs to tell the others.

After this horrifying murder, coupled with an initial retreat of the Allied Forces in view of the sheer force of Hitler's counter-offensive—his last effort to win a war which he could no longer win—General Patton was halted in the European Theater for the first time. Relief came from the First Army advancing to the area. The German defense broke down.

❖

The Netherlands American Cemetery near Maastricht on the highway to Aachen holds the graves of 8,302 who gave their lives in their country's service in battles of Maastricht, Eindhoven, Nijmegen, Arnhem, Julich, Geilenkirchen, Krefeld, Venlo, Cologne and Wesel. Their gravesites are marked by a simple white cross, which bears their names, hometowns and time of death in battle. Of the total, 106 are Unknowns, whose remains were never positively identified.

Most of the soldiers buried here gave their lives in the airborne and ground operations to liberate eastern Holland during the advances into Germany over the Roer River and across the Rhine. In no less than forty instances, brothers lie side by side; one headstone marks the grave of two Unknowns.

I stood in silence when I visited the site in April 2008. While memories welled up in my mind, I placed seven red roses at the cross marking the site of fallen Louis F. Schmidke – TEC 3 Maint Div –Missouri, June 20, 1945. He obviously died after the war ended, most likely from the wounds of battle. He was the last soldier buried at the cemetery.

❖

General Patton was then called to the office of the Allied Supreme Commander, General Eisenhower, near Reims, France. There, in the presence of General Omar Bradley, in charge of all American Ground Forces in Europe and Patton's immediate superior, decisions were made to end this brutal war instantly and at all cost, to defeat Hitler and the German Military Forces to the point of complete and unconditional surrender.

Patton was ordered to regroup, restock food, guns, ammunitions and supplies, and lead his 3rd Army through Belgium and the southern tip of Holland across the German border to the Rhine. We heard the details on the short wave.

"Patton outsmarted Hitler," said Timo von Sachsen, huffing from running back to the living quarters. "I just came from the tunnel and heard it on BBC. He is in Remagen, south of Bonn, waiting to cross the Rhine River. The Wehrmacht has blown up all the bridges across the Rhine, from the Swiss border to Rotterdam, except the one at Remagen. The BBC guessed Hitler needed that one for his retreat to the river's east bank. But Patton's troops got a tip from a German prisoner that it would be blown up by the Wehrmacht in forty-five minutes, at exactly 1600 hours."

"What happened?" we shouted in chorus, leaning forward and hoping for some good news.

"The American Army raced to the bridge. Except for two small demolition explosions, the span across the swollen Rhine was saved. As a result, only some minor repairs needed to be made, which will take about a week."

"So the Americans will come across now?"

"Yes," added Timo, still breathless, "and Hitler called for an instant court-martial of four of the German officers in charge of the bridge. The court was hastily gathered to oblige the already raging dictator and lasted not even an hour. Then all four were executed on the spot for treason."

So the often impatient Patton had to wait until he could cross and march east toward Berlin for what he had hoped and expressed to General Eisenhower as the only way to end the brutal six-year war. But the Supreme Commander was adhering to the Yalta Conference agreement two months earlier, where it was decided that the western Allies would halt at the Elbe River 120 km west of the German capital.

So Eisenhower turned Patton down and ordered him to lead the 3rd Army south to Bavaria and Austria. But once across the river to its east bank and before he followed those High Command orders, he quickly formed a small, special contingent of tanks and artillery to head straight east from Remagen to a place he had heard his son-in-law was kept as a POW: Walthausen, about 300 km further east. The Wehrmacht was already in a rapid retreat after the Americans came across the Rhine, so the special contingent hit little resistance. Patton's tanks roared through with little gunfire.

That evening at midnight, Malcolm jubilantly reported the incident: "Today, Ladies and Gentlemen, a genius has blown the German defense into the dust. Patton's special detachment has secretly reached the POW camp in Walthausen, where over 4,000 American prisoners were kept. The tanks eliminated all the German guards, shot open the gates, and thousands of cheering but starving GIs streamed out and hopped on top of the tanks, hoping for a ride west to safety. It was General Patton's master stroke," Malcolm added with genuine pride.

"Not all American POWs made it to the Rhine," he continued. "When the Germans got wind of the action, they mustered the remains of their Wehrmacht to catch those who were walking west, many without shoes, many even without socks, all without food and water. They were put back into camp—and, as one must assume, were not treated very well after this action."

But as history unfolded, the POWs were freed two weeks later by the advancing Ninth Army.

FRENCH TROOPS ARRIVE
AT UMKIRCHH

꿎

In mid April, units of the French Army crossed the Rhine at Strassbourg, 250 miles further south of Remagen, and ultimately occupied the southwestern portion of Germany. They arrived in Umkirch on April 27, 1945.

That same afternoon, a contingent of at least twenty soldiers led by a sergeant came over to the castle, tried to open the front door, which was locked, then used their rifle stocks to break the door down. They fanned out inside and rounded up all of us: house servants, Frau Möeller, and the nine of us. Each soldier grabbed one of us, using his gun poked into our backs to drive us out of the building through the broken-down front portal. Then they made us lie face down on the graveled circular driveway, stepping their boots on our backs to hold us down. We felt the cold metal of the gun barrels at the backs of our necks.

Ten more soldiers came with ropes to tie us up, feet together first, then hands in our backs. If we would have really tried to move—and indeed I did—the gun barrel in our neck would be pressed harder on our spines.

Fritz tried his French to speak up first. "Je suis le Prince de Hohenzollern, un cousin de la Famille Bourbon." The soldiers didn't move.

Then I spoke up: "Je suis Americain, Messieurs. Je demande un retour a la maison toute suite, s'il vouz plait." The soldiers laughed and rattled an answer to me in a heavily-accented French I didn't understand.

Time stopped. The soldiers obviously debated what to do with us: kill us, or just dump us into the pond with our hands and feet tied together. I understood enough of their heavily dialected language to catch on; yet there was nothing anyone could do at that moment. "Let's just be nice to them, although it's hard to do," I whispered to Fritz, lying next to me.

More time went by. It seemed to me they were waiting for their officer in charge to return and give them orders what to do.

Then I heard footsteps. Many footsteps. A whole horde of footsteps. Oh God, please, not more soldiers! The marching sound came closer, then stopped. And a French voice said loudly and clearly: "NON! Free them! We were treated well by them. We were fed well. Don't touch this family," they chanted in unison. "Let them go back to their house unharmed."

By God! These were our farmhands, the French prisoners of war. And I thought they had all left because the French troops immediately set their prisoners free. But the latter didn't leave. Instead, when there were rumors flying that the Hohenzollerns would have to face charges of forced slave labor, the twenty or so former prisoners decided to stay and stand up for us.

It worked. THEY were our real protectors.

At that time, it never occurred to me that five years later I would be a staunch *Frankophile*.

But with their arrival, I had my freedom back. I could also help protect Fritz, all of my other buddies in our group, Frau Möller and her team of servants and the farmhands from any attempt of further harassment. And it came, but not from the French troops. It arrived not from French officers or soldiers, but foremost from prisoners of war from eastern countries, who had been cut loose by the American and French Armies and were marauding through all of Germany, stealing, threatening, killing.

And who defended us from their invading the mansion, to rob and steal us blind, mistreat, or possibly even kill us?

You guessed it: the French prisoners of war, en masse!

Near midnight three days later, on April 30, we were in the tunnel again. Rumors were spreading the war might soon be over. Indeed, there was BBC announcing that *der Führer* had taken his life by shooting himself with a pistol into his mouth. It was reported to have happened in his bunker under the Chancellery in Berlin, in the presence of his former mistress Eva Braun, whom he had married the day before. She was given poison by the guards to take her life. Hitler had apparently also ordered his guards to poison his favorite German shepherd. Before he shot himself, he appointed in writing a successor in Grand Admiral Karl Doenitz to govern the "Reich" and be Supreme Commander of all its Armed Forces.

❖

Sixty years later, during the summer of 2005, the Germans produced a documentary DVD movie titled "DER UNTERGANG" ("DOWNFALL"), describing the Führer's demise and featuring the Swiss actor Bruno Ganz playing the role of Hitler.

❖

During the May 2005 observance of the sixtieth anniversary of V-E Day, an Associated Press reporter located a former SS bodyguard of Hitler in Berlin. Then twenty years old, he reportedly witnessed some of his SS colleagues, including Bormann, Hitler's valet and a surgeon, enter the Führer's bunker, drag out the bodies of the self-proclaimed leader and Eva, both draped in white bed sheets, into the courtyard of the Kanzlei, drop them into a hole dug by a Russian shell, pour gasoline over the bodies and burn them. The young soldier then feared that he'd be shot as a material witness to the scene and began hiding in dark corners of the huge building until the Soviets came in and took him prisoner.

SURRENDER

❧

On May 6, 1945, Field Marshal Alfred Gustav Jodl and two of his aides were flown by the U.S. Army Air Forces (USAAF) American pilot John T. "Jack" Race from an airport south of Hamburg to Rheims, France. William F. Hallstead, acclaimed writer of over twenty-two books and 400 articles and stories, described this event best in his article "Flight to Surrender the Thousand-Year Reich" published in the May 1999 issue of *Aviation History*. What follows are a few actual quotes from the article, along with a paraphrase of Hallstead's words:

On that day, the most dramatic event of Jack Race's career took place when he flew the German surrender delegation. "We took off from Venlo, in southeast Holland, in our Douglass C-47B code-named Bluenose B for Baker at about 11:00 a.m," he recalled. "My crew consisted of a co-pilot, a flight engineer and a radio operator. My passengers were British Field Marshal Sir Bernard Montgomery's chief of staff Maj. Gen. Sir Francis de Guingand and three of his aides. The weather was not charming at all: low ceiling, reduced visibility, rain."

An hour and forty minutes later Bluenose B touched down at Lüneburg, a north-central town on the Ilmenau River south of Hamburg. As Race taxied the C-47 toward the three waiting German officers, they took on stiff, formal stances. "The balding, bony-faced 56-year-old Jodl was a typical Prussian, straight as a ramrod and rigid in his movements. He really was a commanding presence."

When de Guingand and his aides stepped down from the C-47 and approached the surrender delegation, the Germans saluted smartly—not the outthrust stiff-armed Nazi adaptation of the ancient Roman Legionnaire's salute, but the traditional German Army style. The British officers returned the salute. Then, unexpectedly, stone-faced Jodl stuck out his hand. "The scene," Race recalled, "had a touch of surrealism." There was an embarrassing pause, and then de Guingand stepped forward and shook the defeated general's hand.

At that juncture, according to the radio operator, a peculiar little sideshow took place. "A fighter pilot from Australia tried to hitch a ride with us and he started berating the general (Jodl) as he approached the plane. One of the English officers told him to shut up." The Australian complied and the Germans climbed aboard.

430 miles southwest at Rheims, France, in the strobe-like glare of flashbulbs, Jodl stepped from the Bluenose to surrender what was left of the Third Reich's armed forces. At 2:41 a.m. the next day, May 7, 1945, in a nondescript Rheims schoolhouse, Jodl and the other two members of the German delegation, Admiral Friedeburg and Maj.Gen. Wilhelm Oxenius, signed the unconditional surrender document. General Eisenhower refused to attend in person. Instead, he sent British, French, Soviet and American emissaries to accept the unconditional surrender of all German forces to both the Western Allies and the Soviet Union, together and simultaneously.

Afterwards, Jodl is reported to have said: "With this signature, the German people and armed forces are, for better or worse, delivered into the victors' hands."

The Germans were then escorted to Eisenhower's office and asked by the Supreme Commander if they understood what they had just signed.

"Ja," answered Jodl.

The western participants in the ceremony did not comment.

As the Soviets insisted, the surrender ceremony was repeated the following day, May 8, 1945, in Berlin. There Marshal Zhukov signed for the Soviet Union. So that day became V-E Day and thus the official end of the war in Europe.

Hitler's glorious "1000-year Third Reich" had ended. Begun on January 31, 1933, when he came to power, it had lasted merely a dozen years.

❖

After the surrender ceremony, General Jodl was imprisoned in Spandau, a part of Berlin, until he and twenty other surviving military and civil members of the Third Reich were brought before the Allied Tribunal for War Crimes in Nuremberg, a city located in the American sector 174 kilometers (109 miles) north of Munich.

On October 18, 1945, Allied prosecutors indicted them for crimes against humanity. Seven months later, ten of the twenty-one were sentenced to die by hanging. Jodl was among them. Apparently he wrote his wife a letter with this still-defiant comment: "I have not merited this fate. Death will find no broken, penitent victim, but a proud man who can look him coldly in the eye." (Ich habe den Tod nicht verdient. Der Tod wird mich nicht zerbrochen oder verzweifelt finden. Ich sehe ihm kalt in die Augen.)

A year later, on October 16, 1946, Jodl and the other nine were hung on black-painted gallows in the Courthouse Gymansium. Their bodies were cremated and their ashes strewn into a river near Munich.

When I undertook an extended summer trip to Europe in June 1992, I spent two days in the Bavarian capital that I had always enjoyed. When I became tired from being on my feet for a long time, equally tired from the intense absorption of things to be seen, I scheduled a stop at the Hofbrauhaus, the city's most prominent beer hall, and ate Weisswürste for lunch, a Bavarian specialty of spiced sausages served with potato pancakes and radies, a larger version of our radishes. To wash it down, a one-liter stein of Pschorr beer on draft was placed in front of me by the deft waitress, who asked questions I could not understand. Yet, beer she and I both understood well, as the word is used in both English and German.

Except that I wanted a small glass but instead got a liter stein, the only size they have. It was hot that day and tasted so good that I had a second stein of the golden liquid, the city's famous brew.

Then I reminisced. On my way over here from Salzburg, I remembered, I had gotten off the train in Prien, at the shores of the Chiemsee, a large body of water in the Bavarian foothills at the edge of the Alps. It lies at about 1600 ft above sea level and measures six miles in length and nine miles in width, giving it thirty-three square miles to its own. It is fed by the river Alz, which comes down from the Austrian glaciers. Three islands adorn it on its western side: the 'Fraueninsel' (Lady's Island), 'Herreninsel' (Gentleman's Island) and 'Krautinsel' (Cabbage Island). Each of the first two has had a monastery built on it, appropriately for nuns and monks respectively. The third served both islands as a vegetable patch. Rumor has it that the monks tried to bore a tunnel under the lakebed to reach the nuns without being noticed.

Anyway, I took the ferry over and strolled on the islands for a while, observing in awe the huge castle King Ludwig, the last Bavarian ruler, erected on the Herreninsel, close to the former monastery. He never used it because he died before it was finished.

The Fraueninsel looked nicer, featuring a small village of homes painted with religious figures as is customary in Bavaria. It also has a small marina with fishing boats bobbing on the tiny waves, and an old church that served the nuns when the monastery was still in use.

In a graveyard surrounding it on three sides, I found a large tombstone with the inscription: "Jodl, General of the German Army, born 1895, died 1946."

"He was a good soldier who did his duty. They shouldn't have hanged him.

He did nothing wrong," said the man who had come up to my side. He wore a Loden topcoat and a Bavarian hat featuring an ornate, brush-like beard of a mountain grouse. He spoke the dialect of the area but appeared to be an educated person, obviously a representative of Bavarian high society.

"But he was accused and found guilty of war crimes in Nuremberg in 1945/46," I answered, "was he not?"

"He was, but the Allies convicted him for something he hadn't done." His reply came across angrily.

Historic events flashed through my mind. Wasn't he involved with the concentration camps? Didn't he employ by force eastern laborers to work in Germany's wartime industries? Was he not one of Der Führer's closest confidants? But I could not prove any of it then. I had drawn my knowledge from hearsay or more likely from the BBC news, which tended to overstate. Yet, I felt strongly that I had to challenge this man:

"How do you know that? Did you serve under General Jodl?"

"No, but I know it's true. Everybody here believes he was hanged for no good reason. But I guess that is the victor's prerogative," he countered with a fair amount of spite in his voice.

"Well, that is news to me," I answered, "I don't think the Allied Tribunal in Nuremburg would have sentenced innocent people to death."

He glanced at me, gave me a defiant look and spoke no more. He walked away, as erect as a German high-ranking officer in retirement would do.

I stood motionless for a while, trying to sort out the idiosyncrasies of war, then turned away myself and moseyed over to the restaurant by the water, to eat a fabulous lunch and drink more steins of Pschorr than I should have.

CAPTAIN ANDERKOFFER
A SAINT

The war was over.

The madman from Austria, the paper hanger who declared himself the Führer of the Third Reich, who ruled Germany with an iron fist, who terrorized the world and whose reign to his ultimate demise cost the world millions of money and even more millions of lives—Adolf Hitler was dead.

The preceding twelve years were at first full of promises, of great social reforms idealistically conceived. Six years later, it had all turned into violence, power, killing, shooting, guns, pistols, bombs, raids, casualties, destruction, hunger, sweating, freezing, frostbites, deceptions, cheating, lying, rockets, jets, concentration camps, pursuit of Jews, pursuit of enemies of the State, and senseless murder.

But there was kindness during and after all this turmoil. Silent kindness not written about. Kindness not boasted about. To mind comes the tremendous relief effort of the neutral Swedes in sheltering refugees, in helping others to escape. To mind comes Holland, which helped to receive and hide thousands of Jews who could no longer leave Europe's mid-continent and were harbored by the Dutch in their attics or basements.

My late wife Hanna had told me the story often: her father was a prominent attorney in Berlin who, in the end, became a member of the underground to topple Hitler. In 1937 he had already bought a farm in Bavaria, expecting what Hitler maintained would never happen: a massive war. Hanna was six years old when that war broke out. Long before that, she had been transported to the family's Bavarian farm into safety. That's where she spent the war years with eight of her nine siblings.

Already before Germany surrendered on May 8, 1945, the American 3rd Army had arrived and occupied her part of Bavaria. And soon thereafter, a platoon of American soldiers under the command of a captain came around to the farm, to see if they could use the expansive farmhouse as quarters for the troops, or perhaps for the officers. They spent half a day there. While the captain conferred with his superiors on the phone, the GIs stripped their uniforms, and with rambunctious, youthful noise and energy hopped naked into the lake that was part of the farm.

After about an hour, the captain rounded up his troops and left, but before he mounted his Jeep, Hanna's mother, Countess Astrid, Norwegian by birth, spoke up to him in her fabulously wonderful sing-song accent. She offered him a glass of milk, fresh from the cows in the stable. He politely declined and told his driver to take off.

After that visit, the family was sure the U.S. Army would occupy their farm and chase them away to live somewhere else. Yet no such thing ever happened. Hanna's family always thought the captain was instrumental in that outcome. Because in lieu of sequestering the property, he instead showed up alone two days later, this time driving the Jeep himself. He saluted when Countess Astrid opened the front door and asked if he could now have that glass of milk she had offered.

Thus began a friendship. During the following two months while he was stationed at the nearby town of Füssen, seventeen kilometers away, he would come every two days as a rule but sometimes even every day. He would be served his glass of milk automatically, without asking for it. He would stay for an hour or so then return to his base. He would often bring food items the farm did not have. He would always have with him a lot of chocolate for the kids. He often brought grapefruit as well, to the amazement of all the nine children who bit into them as into an apple because they did not know any other way. And he obviously enjoyed chatting with the countess in the May sunshine on the open terrace overlooking the Alps ten miles to the south.

During one of these occasions, while they were talking on the patio, a German soldier in well-worn, torn and faded Wehrmacht-green garb rounded the corner of the farmhouse, probably in search of something to eat.

At first when he saw the countess on the patio, he stretched out his right arm straight forward in the compulsory form of greeting under Hitler, and shouted: "Heil Hitler," bless Hitler. Then he saw the brown uniform, stopped in his tracks and quickly turned to run away.

The captain never acknowledged this encounter, pretending he had not seen any of it, but instead only said: "Isn't it a lovely view to the mountains today, Countess?"

Germans at that time were not allowed to leave their homes, except to go to the nearest store. When Hanna's brother Hans came down with a nasty case of tuberculosis, the captain came in the Jeep, made Hans crouch up front under the dashboard next to the passenger seat in order not to be seen, and somehow smuggled him through the Army Post along the way to the one and only hospital in town so Hans could receive instant care. Then he brought the needed medicines every day, as they were not available in Germany at that time. During Hans's three-week stay in the hospital, he ferried the siblings, one each time, back and forth the same way.

It lasted six weeks. Then he no longer came for his glass of milk. An inquiry the countess made with the Mayor of Füssen revealed that his platoon had been moved to Linz, Austria.

A saint had come and gone.

❖

When I married Hanna in 1952, I soon heard the story. She remembered his name as Anderkoffer. And for the next twenty-four years she would often talk about the good deeds of Hauptmann Anderkoffer. The name didn't sound American to me. It would translate to "at the suitcase" and that didn't make sense.

So in 1976, I suggested to her that we try to find the hauptmann somewhere in this country. She was overjoyed. I contacted one of my good buddies in Washington to search for him with the Pentagon and as a clue gave him the 3rd Army and Bavaria in May 1945.

"It may take some time," he said on the phone.

"No problem. Take as long as you need."

He called two months later: "The Pentagon found him. His name is Charles S. Undercover, Captain in the Third Army in Bavaria from late April 1945 to honorable discharge in July of that year. He owns a horse farm in Ohio."

Hanna cried with joy. "Write him," I told her.

"No, I can't do that. He will not remember me. I was so young."

"You were twelve in 1945. That's young but not that young."

She did write. Three handwritten pages. She started her letter: "Dear Captain Undercover, I am sure you don't remember me."

His reply came four days later. It was five pages. It recalled every detail of his stay in Bavaria. He started: "Dear Mrs. Hilger, or am I allowed to still call you Hanna? OF COURSE, I remember you. How can I forget the child Hanna, your blonde braids, your blue eyes, your always present smile? How can

I forget your mom? She was such a gracious lady. Please remember me to her with my kindest regards. And if in Ohio, please stop by with your husband and your children. My wife and our kids would love to get to know you and your husband. And we have a few cows and can offer you a glass of milk."

We never did. We thought it best to let the past be as it was.

Heartwarming!

MONSIEUR LE GENERAL
TAKES UP RESIDENCE

A week after the war ended, a French Army Jeep rolled up the circular driveway to Umkirch Castle. The advance team for the general had arrived. They told us without any courtesy introduction to clear Umkirch and gave us twenty-four hours to do so.

We scrambled to pack our stuff. The following day at early dawn, all of us moved out across the field to the farm where, centuries before, a house had been built next to the stables and barns, to serve as the residence for the administrator of the farm operations.

The ten of us moved into one bedroom upstairs that barely held six beds. All of us agreed Fritz, as our master, should have one bed and Albert the other, because he rarely washed. The eight others of us had to double up in the four remaining beds. The only other bedroom next door was occupied by Frau Möller and her female staff. We shared the downstairs living area with some farmhands and the male servants, who slept in the stables or barns or, if unoccupied, the small abodes available for the farmhands.

For our toilet, we used the pig pen. For washing, the small trough outside, near the horse stables, was the spot. For more thorough cleaning after a hot day in the fields, we just walked over to the next pond one-half kilometer away at the edge of the royal forest and took a mostly noisy and joshing-each-other skinny dip in its water warmed by the mid-May sun. We were an extremely good-natured bunch of guys who had become close friends through difficult, life-threatening experiences shared.

Except, maybe, for Albert Joshua. Ever since he joined our group shortly after I did in late November, he was aloof. He invariably displayed an attitude of being something better than we were. He stood to the side. He pitched in with the daily work only if he absolutely had to and then with a visible attitude of defiance written all over him.

He would even defy Fritz, whom all of us considered our master—our *primus inter pares*—by telling him he had cleared his position with the *Fürstin*. He didn't exactly make it easy for the rest of us to like him.

When we were all still in the castle, he had his own room, so his lack of personal hygiene did not directly affect us. But that was different now that we were cramped together into extremely tight quarters. We would call out to him in the morning when we woke up and the stale air from ten guys sleeping hung heavy in the room: "Albert, you stink. Go downstairs and wash!"

At first he did not obey but soon learned we meant every word of it when the nine of us surrounded his bed, threatening to carry him downstairs and dunk him in the trough. From that moment, he began to wash but still refused to skinny dip in the pond with us. But hey, peer pressure will invariably do the job.

Albert left us in June to join relatives in Switzerland. They had obtained a visa for him.

Over at the castle, the Hohenzollern colors were lowered, then the Tricolore raised on the flagpole on top of the tower. The Supreme Commander of the French Occupation Forces, Le General du Corps d'Armee Emil Sevez, had taken up residence. Sentries guarded the wrought iron entrance gate to Umkirch mansion. We were not allowed to get back onto the premises. Not even Fritz, although the general was alleged to be a friend of the French Royal Family Bourbon.

But leave it up to the *Fürstin*. When she heard about it in Sigmaringen through a letter from Fritz, she asked her chauffeur to stoke a fire in the only family car left, a 1939 Mercedes Turbo, which had been equipped with the same wood stove on its rear bumper as Max, the tractor I drove. She arrived the next day, had her chauffeur drive up to the gate, then gave the sentries an earful of royal talk so that they obediently opened the heavy iron barriers and said: "Mais oui, Madame."

Then from the fence we watched Le General step out of the front portal, gently help her out of the car, kiss her hand and lead her into the mansion.

We never heard what went on inside during their two-hour aperitif session. But we had a hunch our temporary relocation to the farm would be of short duration.

A day later, I had my twenty-second birthday. I thought nobody would notice but it turned out everyone knew. For breakfast, Frau Josefine Möller brought a birthday cake into the dining room. She put no candle on it, as they weren't available yet. It was baked from potatoes, nuts from the trees in the park, some lard to keep it from sticking to the baking pan and artificial sweetener.

Fritz lifted his cup of coffee—muckefuk, we called it because it had no caffeine—and said: "Good health." Eight others fell in and we all feasted on cake rarely had. Then it was off to work for all of us. The *Fürstin* was still asleep. But she caught me at lunchtime when I had briefly returned to load up on more wood chips for the Farrell tractor.

"Happy birthday, Gerd. And I brought a small present for you from Sigmaringen. It is something my father was given on a state visit to Serbia shortly before World War I. I want you to have it because you help so much on the farm, get us things we cannot get. And you are such a wonderful friend to Fritz."

With this, she thrust a long object into my hand and continued: "Be careful. It's sharp."

"Thank you, *Fürstin*," I stammered, blushing as my ears burned hot.

It turned out to be a sixteen-inch long knife featuring an ornate wide blade as sharp as a machete, mounted in a short, contoured ivory handle. Both blade and handle showed signs and scripts in Serbian. Even the *Fürstin* did not know what they meant. But the one on the blade's reverse side I could read: SARAJEVO 1896.

The knife is now stationed behind a row of books near one of my night tables. Burglars, beware!

Late that evening, the *Fürstin* had already retired to her quarters for the duration of her short visit, the pantry near the kitchen of the farmhouse. The nine of us sat around our crowded bedroom upstairs. We thought the *Fürstin* wouldn't hear us down in her cubbyhole next to the kitchen. So we turned our crackly old radio up in volume, as loud as it would go.

The American Forces Network (AFN) had just opened up its recording studios in Munich, Bavaria. And that night's program was all "The Big Sound," the big bands playing jazz so extremely well disciplined, sounding as if it was one instrument instead of fifty. The band's conductor was Gene Krupa. I heard his band play again two years later at the Munich Opera, where USO sponsored a well-attended performance.

But that evening in May of 1945, he and the band mostly played, except when Louis Armstrong came on, giving us our first real exposure to Dixie from the Big Easy.

We were—all nine of us—huddled near the radio, tapping our feet in tune with the rhythms, when suddenly the *Fürstin* stormed in, wearing a flowing, long silk morning robe, its borders lined with narrow strips of white mink fur. She looked absolutely and serenely royal.

"What are you boys doing so late at night? And that screeching noise from the ancient radio! I hear it all the way down into the pantry and can't sleep. What's that music anyway? If you listen to that kind of music—that's dance music, YOUR kind of dance music—you ought to dance to it, not just sit around and tap your feet. What YOU are doing is just masturbating."

"M O T H E R!" shouted Fritz.

But his outburst was soon drowned in a roar of laughter that came down from nine twenty-something, red-blooded, healthy, happy and horny bucks. So Fritz joined in as well.

I adored the *Fürstin*, mother of seven herself. All of us non-Hohenzollerns called her *prima primissima*, Latin superlative for "absolutely tops." Today's youngsters would dub her "cool."

MY OPEL
OUR LIFE SAVER

✌

On May 9, 1945, I went over to a farmer whom I had known since I came to Umkirch, and asked him if he would sell me his 1936 Opel P4. He had hidden it from Hitler's agents in his barn. He hadn't driven it since 1939. It was in excellent shape. I offered him Reichsmark 1,000.00, by then only about 120 dollars, and he took it at once. Fritz had come with me to help negotiate the deal, but his help wasn't even needed.

We had brought Max the tractor with us to start the Opel. But it sprang to life on its own with a loud bang out of its tailpipe.

I had a car! I was mobile again! The following day I obtained diplomatic license plates and hung the stars and stripes on the antenna. I was elated.

Shortly thereafter, on May 20, 1945, with surrender a mere two weeks before, I cranked up the Opel at four in the morning and drove north on my first post-war trip. Four hours up the road, I was stopped at the border between the French and American Occupation Zones south of Karlsruhe. The sentry in army fatigues looked at my car and the Stars and Stripes emblem on its front bumper and waved me right through. A few kilometers farther, I entered the heavily damaged town and found the local PX after a number of detours through the rubble-strewn streets.

I needed lots of gasoline for my journey and had built a wooden trunk to rest on the foldable luggage carrier in the rear of the Opel. It could carry four U.S. Army steel canisters, commonly known as Jerry cans, built to hold five gallons each. I also stocked up on K-rations and other supplies I needed, including several cartons of Lucky Strike.

So shortly after the war, Germany had not yet officially been divided into four "Besatzungszonen." No German government existed and no German authority prevailed. No German states had been created. It took another four years for the Westdeutsche Bundesrepublik (BDR) to be founded.

The West was territory conquered by the western Allies: the American, English and French troops. The East was held solely by the Russians. Berlin was the place where all four powers met, to celebrate VE-Day. The Potsdam Agreement happened in June of 1945 only to discuss and decide the fate of the city. But no one then expected it would become a divided city.

The Opel needed gas. A few kilometers out of Karlsruhe on the two-lane Chaussee to Heidelberg, I stopped on the side of the road near a cornfield freshly planted, retrieved a Jerry can from my storage bin, opened the nozzle and started to pour its red contents into my tank. In those days, European gasoline was refined exclusively as synthetic and colorless, whereas American gas was based on crude oil and displayed a reddish color.

Looking down as I poured, I noticed the appearance of a pair of shoes through my spread legs, behind my heels. Highly polished, reddish shoes they were. I knew who was wearing these shoes, but I continued to pour until the tank was full, then lifted the can up, parked it on the ground and closed its lid.

"Now son, where do you think you got that gas from, I might ask?" said the booming voice attached to the polished shoes. I was looking straight into the face of an American Army captain, impeccably dressed and no longer in his battle fatigues. His Jeep and driver were parked on the street in a way that blocked my car.

"I obtained it from the PX in Karlsruhe, Sir."

"And what entitles you to such privileges?"

"This," I said, thrusting my birth certificate forward for him to grab and read.

He did then said. "This does not clearly state you are an American. It says you are the son of an American father, is that correct?"

"Yes, Sir, it is."

"So I am going to ask you to follow me to our Army Headquarters in Heidelberg so that we can verify your status with Washington."

"Okay, Sir. I'd be obliged," I responded, attempting to be as polite as I could.

Trying to verify my status with Washington? Knowing how the government works? How slow they are to react? I am going to be here for days, I thought.

In a small boardroom at Heidelberg's largest downtown building commissioned from the Germans for that purpose, they interrogated me for an hour. Every ten minutes, someone else appeared to ask me the same questions again—and again and again. I knew that was an old, often-used trick to get the truth out of criminals. But I was not a criminal and over a much appreciated great number of fresh donuts with coffee, I held steadfast to what I had told them. They finally gave up, showed me the way to the employee lounge, where I could relax and read the latest issue of LIFE while I munched ham and cheese and pastrami sandwiches and washed them down with Coke. I gladly accepted all of it.

About three or four hours later, the original interrogator came back into the lounge and said: "You are cleared and ready to roll. Washington okayed it. You should now apply for your U.S. Passport. Your father's papers are not totally acceptable for crossing the German border into other countries. Here are application forms issued by the State Department. Fill them out and bring them back here. We will forward them by courier mail. Be sure you include your residence address in there, though, in case we have more questions for you."

A U.S. Passport! Yeah, I needed that. Painful flashes of the Swiss Consulate in Frankfurt seven months earlier flashed through my mind. I still wondered if the man who served me had survived.

"Sure, sir, I'd be obliged. And thanks again for your help."

"You are quite welcome. But I have one more problem with you."

My heart began to sink. "What's that, Captain?"

"We searched your car and found this stack of mail in the glove compartment. Looks like letters to private citizens, all German names and addresses in what is now the British sector. You know we are not allowing anyone to leave their sector to go to another sector. That of course does not apply to you. Nor do we permit the exchange of mail from one occupation zone to the other. And that DOES apply to you. So what's going on here?"

"Sir, you surely know that so shortly after the war ended the German mail system is not yet working again. I have lots of friends where I currently live, near Freiburg, where the French came to occupy their portion of Germany. They all have relatives in the Rhineland, where I am planning to go from here. And they all wanted me to relay their messages to their loved ones that they are alive and okay. Now I am sure you find that all right under these extreme circumstances, don't you, Sir?"

He hesitated a moment, then grinned and said: "Okay, son, I'll let it go this time. But better not do it again, okay?"

"Okay, Sir. I won't. And thanks for your understanding."

"Wait, son! You need more gas? You can go downstairs to the garage. I can phone them."

I chuckled with delight when I replied: "No thank you, Sir. As you know, I just filled up."

"Yeah, I do," he grinned and turned to go back to his office.

Before I left, I went down to the Opel in the parking lot, retrieved a bottle of wine from under the passenger seat, climbed upstairs again, waited in the hall until he had gone to a meeting then placed it on his desk.

On the way to the Rhineland, I crossed from the American Sector to the British. Meanwhile, I had hidden all the mail I carried way under the rear seat among lots of junk, like tools, dirty rags, empty beer and wine bottles and crumpled paper packs of former Lucky Strikes. So the Brits didn't ask and didn't discover.

I crossed the Rhine westward at Remagen to go to the river's left bank. The bridge was the one Patton had repaired a month before. And there, I witnessed, on the railroad tracks leading south to Koblenz and up the Mosel river into France, the plundering of the coal trains.

The "victorious" French, who had really not contributed that much to the war effort but were tolerated by the Americans and British, insisted that they were to be compensated for their contribution with coal from the still rich underground reserves the Ruhr district could yield. They requested the British Army to have the Germans load train after train and send them south and west to France. Good-natured as they were, the Brits obliged.

Was it perhaps that the French still remembered the Germans driving them out of the Rhineland, and thus the Ruhr district, after five years of occupation in 1923?

But what they never found out—or knew but purposely ignored—was the often used practice of the German engineers operating the steam locomotives of those trains to stop in front of signals that they, when questioned, claimed were red. Hordes of German citizens waiting by the tracks climbed into the open gondolas with their buckets to fill as much as they could carry to heat their homes and kitchen stoves. Others would just shovel the black diamonds down onto the tracks for later retrieval. After five minutes, the engineer would blow the engine's horn twice, a signal for everybody to jump down and off, and the long train would start moving again. This ritual was repeated in the suburbs of many more towns in the British occupation territory, but when the train entered the French Zone, their army would not tolerate such practice and stopped it quickly.

I felt for the Germans. They were so poor, cold and starving. I threw them some packs of Lucky Strike from the open car window. They smiled a sincere *"Danke schön"* before I left. The smell of raw coal followed me for quite a few kilometers.

MARAUDING RUSSIANS

A few kilometers north of Remagen lay Rolandseck, a charming village on the banks of the Rhine looking across to the "Siebengebirge," the seven mountains. That's where the mother of my longtime friend Klaus lived. Her name was Erika, and I decided to visit her. When there, I would ask her if I could sleep on a blanket spread out on her living room floor.

I found her stately villa without a problem. It was owned by Erika's British parents who, as a result of the raging war, had not been there since 1939. The village had been saved from air raids and looked intact, albeit run-down. When Erika opened the front door, I found her unchanged: a very tall, elegant and attractive lady with coal-black hair, bright brown eyes and a constant smile. She was thinner than I remembered her, likely because food was so scarce in Germany during the six-year war and especially now so shortly after the surrender.

When I hesitatingly launched my inquiry as to whether I could stretch out on her living room floor, she said: "Nonsense." She pointed upstairs, "Klaus has another bed in his room. That's where you sleep."

"You mean he is here? I thought Hitler drafted him to man the flak guns to shoot down B-24s."

"He is. He came home a week ago. He was captured by the British, became a prisoner of war but was released early because he was so young, only sixteen. I'll get him to come down."

"No need for that," I said, already heading for the staircase. "I know where his room is. Been there often." Then I ran up, taking steps two at a time.

My buddy was stunned and silent at first when I stormed into his room without knocking. But he quickly recovered from the surprise, and a highly emotional reunion followed with my friend from past childhood years. Shaking hands, backslapping, embracing, roughhousing—all of that lasted quite a while until we settled down to talk. In earlier years, I probably was his role model. He had often told me so. I still seemed to be. We had not seen each other for more than six years. We had a strong bond then and still do at the time of this writing, so many decades later.

Over dinner of boiled potatoes and leafy cabbage, and later during the long evening's course of conversation, Erika told me that her husband was sighted near Erfurt, in the Soviet occupation sector. "I am so worried. But I am excited also. Perhaps he is alive," she said desperately. "Can you help us? You know we Germans are not allowed to travel. You have all the papers and a car and gasoline, so can I ask you to find him for us?"

"Sure," I said without hesitation. To me, helping her was the most natural thing in the world at that moment. I knew it was risky to go into Russian territory, yet I was sure I would be okay. I had all the papers identifying me as an American, but probably needed more K-rations and definitely gasoline. I was certain the British would help me out.

"Maybe you would take Klaus along for company?"

"Be glad to." That was a more difficult question. He didn't have any papers. He, as a German, was not allowed to travel.

"Do you have any papers?" I asked him, though I knew he didn't.

"No," he said.

"Well, I'll get you through. So let's do it." I wasn't quite certain if it would work. "The worst scenario should be that we return if the Russians don't allow you to cross."

It took two days to unpack the wine and the twelve cartons of Lucky Strike I had brought, planning to barter them after we returned, for nails and tools, things light and small enough for the Opel to carry back to Umkirch. Then we packed again the things we needed going east, like K-rations enough for two weeks. And one carton of the cigarettes went with us as well, for what we thought would be a slim chance we could use as currency on the other side, in Soviet territory. We obtained more general supplies as well—especially more gasoline from the Brits—before we took off.

A day later, we drove the Opel east through the wreckage of war into the Russian occupation zone to try to find his father, a Wehrmacht colonel, who was missing in action but reportedly had been sighted. When his dad was drafted into the German Army, Klaus was only nine years old. One year later, World War II began. Before this time, his father was last seen in the Ukraine near Stalingrad, where some of the worst and bloodiest battles of the war were fought.

I was, of course, free to move about Europe, but Klaus was not. He was five years my junior. I slipped him past the Russian border guards by claiming he was my kid brother. Brother? He had pitch-black hair and brown eyes; mine were blue along with my fire-engine red hair and lots of freckles. The Russians looked at us, then at my papers, which they held upside down. So they couldn't even read! They handed them back to me, shrugged and let us through.

There were no inns, no hotels, no places of lodging at all. Whatever was not bombed out was closed, if for no other reason than lack of guests. There were no restaurants either. We lived on cold food, primarily the K-rations we had taken along.

Occasionally we would pass a small farm and stop to ask for a hot meal. Even farmers didn't have much to eat then. But potatoes with gravy made with flour and nothing else, and some fresh cabbage from the first harvest of the season were almost always available. We paid with a pack of Lucky Strike. They carried the value of a pound of butter. Barter was the currency of the time.

At night, more often than not, we slept on wooden benches in beer saloons after they closed at ten. Sometimes, there was only one bench not even two feet wide, which we had to share to get off the dirty floor.

During the nights, Klaus often got up to smoke a cigarette: Lucky Strike of course, from my supplies.

"You need to move your bones?" I asked.

"Naaa. Just can't sleep." Then he would fall silent again.

"You okay, bud?"

"Yeah."

He wouldn't admit it, but I knew he was deeply troubled. After a while, he would come back and stretch out in our cramped quarters.

Russians in sloppy, drab uniforms were everywhere. They were reported to use the toilet bowls to wash their hair. German policemen in well-worn and faded green uniforms regulated traffic that didn't exist. We were eyed with great suspicion by both. Russians even showed hate in their faces.

The Cold War had just begun!

We spent nearly two weeks crisscrossing Germany's eastern provinces. We followed every tiny lead on our way. We checked out official records in town halls. More often than not, we went door to door, talking to countless people.

"Have you heard of Colonel Klaus Reese?" his son would ask.

They would reply: "No. And we don't care where he is. We have enough trouble just to survive, find food, and hide from the Russians. So don't bother us. Go away."

Indeed, Russian troops were looting, marauding, raping, stealing, killing everywhere. As people had done for centuries before to other people. (As Serbs would do fifty-five years later to Albanians in Kosovo. History has a tendency to repeat itself.)

But now I was seriously worried about Klaus's safety as a West German without any papers. Too much crime and reckless Russian gun-shooting erupted all around us. It could easily involve us, hit us, kill us.

We never found Klaus senior.

On our return trip, the Russians did not want us to leave their newly occupied "workers' paradise," as they called their sector in compliance with Stalin's doctrine of imposing the Soviet Union's social system on every inch of land they had conquered. They retained us for more than five hours at one of only three checkpoints to the west. Although it was a cool spring day, sweat pearled down my forehead. My heartbeat did some unusual dancing from the anxiety.

From their shabby barracks where we were locked inside, we could see the Union Jack flutter in the wind some twenty yards away. We did not know then that those twenty yards would soon thereafter be widened to 100 yards and become a no-man's land, a strip of the earth's surface razed of all vegetation to clearly detect those who would dare to leave their "workers' paradise." Although officially—or so it was stated by the Russians—they cleared the strip to better spot those capitalists from the West wanting to infiltrate their sector of "ideals" and "welfare" for the masses.

Almost seven hours later, we were waved through without an explanation. I have never been happier in my life to see a Brit.

At the end of another month, my mother wrote that her sister's oldest daughter—my cousin Marliese, who lived in Berlin—was raped by six Russian soldiers consecutively, then slit open with a machete from her neck to her abdomen and left to bleed to death.

❖

Klaus and I had been childhood pals. But during that sad excursion, a much closer friendship was cemented. It has lasted to this day—more than six decades!

We get together as often as we can. We are soul mates. Our brotherhood kicks in the moment we see each other at the airport. Our partners in life discreetly and politely retreat as we revel in our linkage. He became an architect. With Brigit, he lives in a 123-year old fieldstone farmhouse among olive trees on Spain's Mediterranean island Mallorca. While its outside was left unchanged in compliance with Spanish law, he revamped the inside to sparsely furnished, airy, sunlit living space. He can see the Med's blue-green waters from his patio. Sixty meters down the hill, he built a separate, spacious fieldstone guesthouse. That's where I hang out.

But even now, after so many years, I shudder at the thought of how dangerous it was to take Klaus along to the East.

WHO STOLE THE BONES OF FREDERIK THE GREAT?

I n early June, just two days after I had returned from my hazardous
sojourn into the Soviet Occupation Zone, all of us moved back into
Umkirch Mansion. Monsieur Le General had been offered another,
slightly larger Hohenzollern castle further east, which was not inhabited
at the time and "so much larger and more befitting a general of your
standing," to quote the *Fürstin* as she told us the story later.

"Leave it up to Mother. She'll get it done somehow," Fritz said.

No wonder she had gotten from Hitler pretty well everything she
wanted!

As soon as we were all settled in and had taken possession of our
previous bedrooms, Fritz gathered all of us around one evening and said:
"Guess what. The Americans have retrieved the remains of King
Friederich der Grosse from their resting place at his beloved Sans-Souci
Castle at Potsdam."

"Wow. Why did they do that? Did they dig him up? Where is
Friederich now? In Washington? Did the Americans snatch him?" we
exclaimed all at once.

"No. The American Army brought the leaden casket holding the king's remains to Regensburg. I was told that General Patton is responsible for that. He was known to be a history buff and had likely read the achievements of *Friederich der Grosse* with great admiration."

"Why Regensburg?" we wanted to know.

"Patton had met and gotten to know the *Thurn und Taxis* family during his blitz-like conquest from Remagen down to Linz, Austria. He had sequestered their castle for ten days to live there while the 3rd Army regrouped. He must have asked them if they could store the remains in one of their churches."

"Did they?"

"Yes," Fritz concluded. "The casket is now resting in one of the several deep crypts beneath the Regensburg Cathedral."

"How did you find out about this whole affair?" I asked Fritz.

"My uncle, the *Fürst* of Thurn and Taxis, wrote a letter to my dad. It took several weeks to travel from Regensburg to Sigmaringen. As you know, the postal service has just resumed. The mail is slow also because it has to cross from the American into the French Occupation Zone. So we found out about this development only last week."

I was impressed. The King *Friederich von Preussen* and Prince *Friederich von Hohenzollern* had done a lot of good for the state during his forty-six-year reign. He was called "The First Servant of the State of Prussia." Born in 1712, he came to the throne in 1740 and ruled until his death at Sans-Souci in 1786. He displayed great tolerance toward the religions of his subordinates, adopted measures to advance education of his people, generated farmland by damming the lowlands, and effected many social reforms unheard of in those days.

He also displayed a lively interest in intellectual matters, was an ardent admirer of Voltaire and despised the German language. French was what educated Germans spoke during his term. However, later he wrote that the German language would have a great future. Which it did until WWI.

But he lives on in German history as "The Great," foremost for his achievements for the people, but also his military strength, which guaranteed peace for Prussia.

"So what might have inspired the American Army to rescue his bones?" asked Franz, who normally did not concern himself with matters of intellect.

"They rescued him because he was a German icon, a man becoming a national hero again in Germany. The Allies probably had enough by now of German heroes," said Georg von Mecklenburg, forever our wise and well-read companion.

"And they were probably afraid the Soviets might discover his remains and burn them on the Kremlin Square for all to see," added Max.

And so we theorized for weeks. Finally we moved on to other things of importance. But *Friederich der Grosse* was not forgotten.

❖

In 1946, when things had somewhat normalized in Germany and roads were open and passable again, the Thurn and Taxis family had the casket shipped from Regensburg to the Hohenzollern family in Sigmaringen, where, they rightfully assumed, the King's remains belonged. After all, he was a Prince of Hohenzollern as well.

But the Hohenzollern Burg in Sigmaringen was still occupied by the French. So Fürst Friederich, Fritz's father, had the casket shipped to one of the other castles the family owned, this one in Hechingen, south of Stuttgart. That's where it was placed to rest in the crypt under the chapel.

Years later, during my 2003 visit to Sigmaringen, Fürst Fritz von Hohenzollern, now the head of the family and still my close friend for all those many years, asked me if I could do some research in Washington. I promised I would try.

I went to work on the mystery soon after my return from Europe. But now, so many years later, I found no reference anywhere of the U.S. Army advancing as far as Potsdam. It was earmarked in Yalta as part of the Soviet Occupation

Zone. Situated twenty-five miles west of Berlin on the banks of the river Havel, it had for centuries been the military bastion of Germany and the location of a small castle, Sans Souci, where the King had lived and was buried.

Yet I can't be totally wrong in my assertion that the bones of Frederik the Great were indeed rescued by the American Army. After all, he was a symbol of German Monarchy, of German Militarism, which I am sure the Soviets would have confiscated and/or eliminated by a bonfire on the Kremlin Plaza for the whole world to see.

My theory? Let's go into the known facts of history as they became evident close to the end of WW II, in April of 1945. At that time when the Soviet Armies were still battling with the remainder of the disintegrating Wehrmacht in eastern Poland, the U.S. First, Third and Ninth Armies—all under the command of General Omar Bradley's 12th Army Group—penetrated deep into territory later to become part of the Soviet-dominated East Germany. While the Third under Patton was called back and sent south to Bavaria and Austria, the First and Ninth reached and occupied Magdeburg, Halle, Erfurt, Buchenwald, Stendal, Leipzig, Chemnitz and Dresden.

These conquests were located much further east than the Elbe River—the line through Germany where the Allies should meet—as agreed upon in Yalta in February 1945 by Roosevelt, Churchill and Stalin. And a month after the war ended, General Eisenhower indeed called the troops back to west of the Elbe and beyond. Yet, throughout this period, Patton had prevailed on Eisenhower to let him go all the way to Berlin, but he was ordered to march south. I find no fault in Eisenhower's decision to adhere to the agreement. I had the honor to know the man personally from visits to the White House and Gettysburg. His integrity was outstanding. I find fault only with the loopholes in the Yalta Agreement.

The Supreme Commander and General Omar Bradley knew Patton very well. He was extremely successful, a solid soldier and outstanding commander. But he also had a temper that at times got away with him.

Might Eisenhower have used caution in avoiding a confrontation between

Patton and Soviet Marshall Zhukov in Berlin? Ike got along well with the Russian. As seasoned officers, they were prudent and careful not to interfere with each other. Their aim was to avoid firing at the other when they would meet on the streets of Berlin. The Supreme Commander's strategy was not the glory of marching first into the ruined German capital. His urgent goal was to end the war as soon as he could, to avoid further losses of lives. But unclear to this day is why we did pull back from the Elbe River Line, further west than we had to, and conceding areas we had conquered and which were ours.

In retrospect, I think Patton was right. We lost quite a bit of ground in Yalta with unnecessary concessions made by a dying American President. But our position was strong. Who, after all, financed the Russians with Lend Lease? What would the world look like if we had stayed out of the conflict? Had we marched into Berlin with Patton, Zhukov might have been furious. But the Soviets wouldn't have thrown us out. They understood the language of power. After their huge losses of manpower during the preceding years, they were also glad to end the conflict.

If the western Allies had progressed to the German capital, we would have had a lot fewer problems after the war. Berlin would have stayed accessible to all four powers; the Air Lift lasting from June 24, 1948, to September 30, 1949, would not have been necessary. The Cold War might have turned out less threatening than it did.

All this is hindsight. History chose another way. But to me, it is conceivable that based on the recommendation of Patton—who was everywhere known for his strong nationalism—the Ninth, under the command of Lt. General William Hood Simpson, sent a commando to Potsdam on the mission to retrieve Frederik's remains. During the heavy fighting of November 1944 and during the rapid advance across the plains of northern Germany, the Ninth was the first Allied Army to reach and cross the Elbe River.

On April 12, 1945, Lt. General Simpson had established a firm bridgehead on the eastern banks of the Elbe and was ready to advance the remaining fifty miles to Berlin. At that time, they were north of Magdeburg when Simpson received his orders to cease further advancement east. The Russians were decimated and had not yet arrived in Berlin. What was left of the Wehrmacht was in retreat. For the Ninth, Potsdam was only a few kilometers away, lying there in a vacuum. Patton knew Simpson. They communicated well with each other. Omar Bradley was their commanding general. Both were in touch with him even more.

Can the details of such a mission still be buried deep in some Pentagon and OSS, now CIA, filing cabinets? If they are, the U.S. government has not responded to my inquiries.

But remembering his pledge told in an earlier chapter—un-announced to his superiors—to free his son-in-law along with four thousand other GIs held in a POW camp at Walthausen after he had crossed the Rhine at Remagen, it sounds absolutely plausible that Patton, already on his trek to southern Bavaria and Austria, persuaded his colleague and friend Simpson to do with Frederik the Great's remains what he himself had done to free the 4,000 American POWs. He might have told Simpson: "Bill, this is George. Send in a special commando and get that blasted casket out of Sans-Souci. And ship it to me. I am staying at the castle of the Thurn and Taxis Family near Regensburg. I'll get it into the right hands." That would have been typical of him.

The royal casket remained in the Hechingen crypt for forty-six years. In 1992, three years after the German reunification, and Berlin had again become the capital, the then Federal Government of Germany, still in Bonn, asked for Fritz's permission and release of the royal casket for shipment from Hechingen by special envoy to its original resting place at Sans-Souci in Potsdam. Fürst Fritz von Hohenzollern was the guest of honor and rendered a memorable eulogy at the gravesite.

So Friederich der Grosse was home again.

Later that summer of 2003, I visited Berlin and Potsdam, stepped to the burial site and silently thanked those who saved the remains of the great man.

THE POTSDAM AGREEMENT

꒦꒷꒦

S hortly thereafter, in mid-June 1945, the agreement to divide Berlin was negotiated. It had been planned as a result of discussions held at the summit of the three powers in February 1945 at Yalta, Soviet Union, where Roosevelt, Churchill and Stalin had met to decide post-war arrangements.

As a result, the victorious powers—the United States, Britain and the Soviet Union—met at Caecilienhof, a large castle on the shore of Lake Wannsee west of Berlin. As in Yalta, the Soviets were again the hosts.

Caecilienhof was built by Kaiser Wilhelm II in 1914-1917. The German Kaiser never resided there for any length of time, as he was exiled to Holland soon after the castle's completion. The huge mansion had become part of the Soviet Occupation Zone. Situated on the northern edge of the old military bastion called Potsdam—significantly, only five kilometers away, where the German military had reigned for centuries—the city and the castle were considered symbols of Prussian Militarism.

The Soviets occupied the large buildings and invited the entire delegations of their Allies to stay there as well for the duration of the conference. But tensions had already commenced between Russia and the West. Fearing wire-tapping, the American Army therefore built a pontoon bridge across Lake Wannsee from the western sectors of the city to the Caecilienhof for the daily negotiations so that the western delegations could return to their respective quarters in their zones at night.

The Agreement laid down the structure of the division of the German capital among the four powers. It created the so-called sectors of occupation and specified free access by land and water as well as air routes from Hamburg, Frankfurt and Munich. The soon to be restarted German Airline Lufthansa was not allowed to fly any of those access routes. Only Pan American, British Airways and, a year later, Air France provided air service to the city.

Next to Stalin and Churchill, the American representative now was the new President and Commander-in-Chief from Missouri, Harry S. Truman, who two months later ended the war in the Pacific by dropping two A-bombs on Japan, thus forcing that country to surrender as well.

President Truman reportedly made any and all attempts at reneging on the commitments in Yalta made by the dying President Roosevelt.

But Stalin was a strong, confident victor. He knew what he had achieved and was not willing to concede one inch. His strategy was that every victor in the conflict had the right to impose on its gained territory a social system of his own liking. And Stalin undoubtedly wanted as much territory on its western front as he could possibly muster. Thus he laid the cornerstone for the Cold War.

Consequently, the agreement to divide Berlin became commonly known as the Potsdam Agreement. It was signed by the three powers on August 2, 1945.

France, as a non-participant in Yalta, was not invited but later was assigned a part of the city as their territory from Berlin's western half, that which was assigned to the U.S. and England.

MY TIME AT RUM RUNNING

❧

M y car and my American birth certificate—used until I received
the U.S. passport I had applied for in May with the captain at
the American Forces Headquarters in Heidelberg—gave me a chance to
create a lifestyle for myself and for my protectors, the Hohenzollerns,
which was independent from others. Both enabled me, during the next
three years, to establish a network of sources and outlets for a flourishing
barter trade.

Food was extremely short in all of Germany. Food rationing was still
in place from the war years, yet now there was even less to buy. Long
lines formed in front of empty stores. People sold their silverware for
potatoes or their jewelry for a small piece of meat. Consumer goods were
non-existent. You repaired what you owned.

Whichever industrial plant would reopen and was in need of energy
could not produce, because every day of the week a dozen freight train
locomotives would pull fifty gondolas each of Ruhr coal for the
Occupation Forces or shipment to France.

People in the French and English occupation zones were worse off than
in the American Zone. The American Military Government asked
German officials to come into their offices in Heidelberg to discuss their

food needs. The Americans asked: "What do you need most?"

"*Korn,*" was the answer of the Germans. Consequently, freighter after freighter from the United States arrived in German ports and unloaded tons of corn.

The Germans didn't say much. Corn was *Mais* in German, used mostly as cattle and pig feed. But "korn" was food. And food they needed. German mothers became ingeniously involved in the making of corn dishes such as puddings, veggie casseroles, bread spreads and corn soups.

It was many months later that the Americans found out what happened: *Korn* in German means grain or wheat in English. But the Germans didn't speak any English, so the Americans understood Korn as corn. We had a lot of that in the United States.

But I always had as much gasoline as I wanted, courtesy of the French Army, which honored my status as an American citizen. I never had to pay for it either. And what I didn't need for my Opel, I gave to Fritz. Nails, tools, cutlery and other manufactured goods like lamps, steam irons or shoes could be obtained in Germany's industrialized western part. Clothes were available from the area around Stuttgart.

Not for money, heavens no. But wine from the Kaiserstuhl or butter from the farms in the high mountain meadows of the Black Forest bought a lot of these items that, in turn, were badly needed by the dairy farmers and vintners around Freiburg.

I blessed my connection to the Henkel family in the Kaiserstuhl, a connection which had already started during the preceding winter. They too needed a lot of farm tools and parts for their machinery used to harvest the grapes. And butter to cook, flour to bake and bed linen to sleep in. They became a true and friendly supplier/customer. My source for Kaiserstuhl wine was limitless! When I visited them to trade, I—and Fritz if he came along, which he often did—would always end the encounter with dinner in their elegant dining room before Hector pulled us home, our wagon loaded with our liquid loot.

And so it went: Lucky Strikes for butter,

> butter for nails,
>
> nails for eggs,
>
> eggs for shirts,
>
> shirts for wine,
>
> wine for tools,
>
> tools for butter, etc. etc.

If all else failed, I would run up the fewer than 100 kilometers to Karlsruhe to pay a visit to the local Army PX, where I exchanged dollars for chits and would stock up on such items as difficult-to-get medication, gasoline, of course, and always several cartons of Lucky Strike, the most valuable currency of the day.

"I am a heavy smoker," I would tell the sergeant on duty.

"Yeah, I can see that. You was here just four days ago," he would reply with a wide grin.

And I always made sure that my bartering generated enough of a surplus to help Fritz and the farm with nails, tools, tires and gasoline or diesel, or whatever else he might have needed in items accessible to me.

Looking back, I realize these times of total dependence on each other, of hardships endured, but equally joyful moments shared, formed solid lasting friendships among all of us—but foremost with Fritz, a bond continuing as long as we will live.

The nine of us were basically a bunch of women-less guys. The only exceptions happened when we were in classes at the university. But in those days, the ratio between boys and girls was 88:1. Our chances to find a partner were extremely thin.

No wonder then that I instantly fell in love with Inez Countess Hoyes when she came to visit for a long weekend. Head over heels, I did. She was a member of a well-known Hungarian aristocracy and possessed all the temperament, fierce intensity and charm of southern Europeans, features I knew would make my head spin.

But what I had not known, nor counted on, was that she was Konstantin's girl. He was not there when she arrived and came a day later. He and I had gone through hell together during the preceding year in Umkirch, and we had become buddies. So when he raised his voice somewhat to advise me that Inez was his, I let go. Immediately!

Nevertheless, I kept trying to look for a partner in my life. Or if not in my life, then at least for the time being. Lucky Konstantin, he didn't have to worry about that.

The University of Freiburg opened its doors again and started the first post-war winter semester at the end of October 1945. But quite a few of its faculties could not function yet because the buildings they were housed in were still damaged. I began to commute to campus by car, regularly filled beyond seating capacity with my roommates, many of whom had also enrolled to continue their studies. A few always had to sit on the car's rear luggage carrier, which was doable because the Opel, so old and fragile, was most comfortable with speeds up to 40 Km, 25 mph.

Tuition was the least of my problems. It was charged in the old, wartime Reichsmark currency that deteriorated in value day by day. I still had over 1,000 Reichsmark left in the bank. Tuition for an entire year was charged at less than two hundred marks. But a pound of butter was worth at least five hundred marks—or one pack of Lucky Strike, or whatever other barter objects were worth at that time.

During that first winter back at school, only a few students were registered and attended classes, housed in buildings barely intact and often without heat. On a typical winter day in Freiburg, the temperature could easily fall into the freezing range and stay there all day, all night, all week.

The School of Medicine remained closed until further notice. I enrolled in Economics and Law. That was to change the direction of my life!

Professor Boehm taught me the Bürgerrecht, Germany's famed citizen law, which would prove rather useless for me in my career. Professor Eucken preached Economics. But during these troubled times, I had already learned more about the world of supply and demand through my bartering than I could possibly have acquired from him. He was an acclaimed, aloof, but much admired icon, who specialized in the theories of National Economies.

What he never realized was that barter trade eluded his teachings. That kind of trade was foreign to him, yet it went on right under his nose and was carried out by one of his students. Or maybe he did know that I was deeply involved? Did he know that my friends called me a rum-runner? Did he know more about me than I guessed?

Perhaps he did, because when I graduated, I found out he had recommended me to the French government for a two-year scholarship at La Sorbonne in Paris. I was astonished because my grades at the university certainly did not warrant my being committed to such a distinguished school as the Sorbonne was—and still is.

Whatever he knew, that scholarship carried me through law school.

ESCAPING TO SWITZERLAND

~᭟~

During late spring of 1946—as a matter of fact, it was a few days before my birthday in May—I entered into another venture that I should most likely not have undertaken. As already mentioned, when I made my first trip north a year earlier and was briefly stopped by the U.S. Army in Heidelberg, I had been handed application forms for a U.S. Passport. I filled them out and delivered them to the harsh but good-hearted captain at the Heidelberg U.S. Army Headquarters on my next journey north a few weeks later. I never heard from them again nor did I receive my passport.

So I decided to find my way into Switzerland and travel to the U.S. Embassy in Bern to see for myself what was holding up my papers. That turned out to be a bold move—and a frustrating mistake!

Freiburg was not far from Schaffhausen—the only Swiss city lying on the right bank, and therefore north, of the Rhine River which separated Germany and Switzerland between Lake Constance and Basel. I chose it because the border was on land and not on the center of a bridge across the water. I knew a few unpaved side roads into the city and could use them to avoid the Swiss immigration agents. I was sure that my dad's papers would not be considered valid identification for me to cross the border officially even though my American status would suffice once I was in the country.

At the border, everything went smoothly. Nobody stopped me. No one was there. Some people on the Swiss side slowed down walking when they saw the Opel pass by. I just waved to them and continued on my way. The Stars and Stripes emblems front and rear probably quieted their minds.

I parked the car at the railroad station. There was only a scattering of other cars in sight, because even Switzerland was still recovering from the shortages of war. Inside, I checked the timetable for the next train to Zürich. It was going to leave one and a half hours later, enough time to have a cup of strong coffee and a delicious éclair—things I hadn't been able to enjoy since 1939.

Once settled in the coach, I unfolded the latest copy of the *Zürcher Zeitung*. My reading time didn't last very long. The conductor came by and asked for my ticket.

"So you are going to Bern?" His accent was total and genuine Schwizerdeutsch.

"Ja."

"*Sie müssen umsteigen in einen anderen Zug in Zürich.*"

"*Ja, ich weiss,* I will take the express to Bern when I get there."

"*Sehr gut.*"

He left the compartment and closed the sliding door to the coach's corridor. I returned to reading the paper.

Five minutes later he came back, this time in the presence of a green uniformed Swiss border guard.

"*Papiere, bitte,*" he said curtly.

I shoved my identity card and my dad's citizenship papers over to him. He studied both, then placed them in his leather pouch and said: "I must ask you to come with me to the compartment we maintain on this train.

You don't appear to have the correct papers to enter Switzerland legally. I am not arresting you, but you need to be under our observation and in our custody until we get to Zürich."

"And what will happen there? Can I take my express to Bern?"

"No sir. Another team of our colleagues will escort you back to the border on the next train to Schaffhausen and then to the German border."

"But I left my car at the train station."

"That's okay, as you say. Our people have cars too. We will make sure you exit Switzerland."

"Can I at least phone my embassy in Zürich?"

"Yes, we have phones at the main station at our offices there."

I went with him to the front of the train and settled into the comfortable first class compartment the border guards occupied.

"Sir, would you like to share a sandwich with us? Rye bread with butter and Cervelat sausage? Or Emmenthaler cheese? We also have some lemonade here if you are thirsty. And how about some Lindt chocolate? It's Swiss made. We make it *gut.*"

I hadn't had a lunch like that in over six years!

Once in Zürich, I had a few minutes turn-around time to try the U.S. Embassy, but didn't reach anybody, as it was lunchtime.

I was back in Schaffhausen at shortly after three, retrieved the Opel and returned to German soil twenty minutes later.

So much for trying to cross a border without a passport.

❖

I have traveled to Switzerland numerous times since. Every time I cross the border, I think of this incident—even now as I write this in 2006. The Swiss are not a member of the European Union. They still have the Swiss Franc as their currency. They still require a passport to enter and leave their country.

A FATEFUL JOURNEY
NORTH BY TRAIN

❧

During winter recess, between fall and winter semesters from December 22, 1946, to January 8, 1947, I decided to visit my parents and spend Christmas and New Year with them. They were back in Germany and lived near Cologne at that time, some 550 kilometers north of Freiburg.

My Opel's tires were not that good anymore, and I had great trouble finding new ones because the size of my wheels was outmoded and no longer used by the automotive industry. So I took the train.

Georg brought me to the train station in Freiburg with Hector pulling the by now familiar two-wheeled buggy. I took a local to Frankfurt, a long journey because it seemed to stop at every second barn. In Frankfurt, I could connect to a faster one.

It was marked as an "express" train on the schedule, with limited stops between Frankfurt and Cologne, and drawn by a vintage steam locomotive, which was "speeding" along at sixty kilometers—less than forty miles—per hour. Its eighteen coaches wound around picturesque hills, now in the dark of that winter night, bordering the river Rhine on its eastern side. The train was packed. Already, when I boarded in

Frankfurt two hours earlier, there had been hardly any standing room left.

At first I stood wedged into people around me in the aisle. I knew not much could happen as I was cushioned by a lot of bodies. Later, I managed to squeeze myself into a tight spot near a door. I considered myself lucky to have found it after another passenger departed at the station we had just left. People stood on the couplings between the coaches and hung on to the bumpers with their hands numb from the cold.

Two days before Christmas!

My backpack held a couple of bottles of exquisite wine from the *Kaiserstuhl* Mountains. I had bartered them during an earlier visit to my friends Lisa Henkel and her husband Dr. Pettersen for two packs of Lucky Strike. I knew that my father would enjoy the wine. He drank a glass every evening with supper.

Near Neuwied, a small town almost opposite Koblenz, on the Rhine River, it all of a sudden happened: I heard a loud thump. Then a few seconds of silence. Then a jerking forward motion of our coach. Then earsplitting screeching set in, followed by intense whining.

The train's motion knocked me off my feet, forward in the aisle, leaning on others already on the ground, then sideways into the first compartment, filled with eight passengers and numerous others, like me, thrown into the tight spaces and on top of everyone else. Our coach had started to gradually lean over to the right, swaying as it did so.

When it reached an angle of over ninety degrees, it jerked forward some more, then, with heavy metal bending and glass shattering from the impact's force, it slid down the embankment and came to rest on the street below.

In seconds it was over. Then silence—deep silence at first! At least, that's what I felt. But I may have been knocked unconscious by the catastrophic terrors around me.

I awoke to the screams of human voices. Ear-piercing they were. Above all, I heard the sinister sound of the locomotive's steam hissing out of its damaged boiler, its horn blowing loudly, and incessantly.

In the human chaos inside our coach, people trampled other people. Some were already dead or would die soon from hundreds of feet walking over and crushing them. Men and women screamed for help. But those that could climbed out through broken windows, most of their glass shattered away, on the aisle side of the coach, ripping bloody their arms, legs and faces, tearing their clothes, hoisting themselves up either alone or with pushes from others behind them, aiming for the dark night sky above them, not aware of its wintry, starry beauty.

My head was bouncing, throbbing. I had blood running down my face. I had no chance to discover where it came from. There was no time to worry now about a wound on my head certain to continue bleeding. Out, out I must go. NOW! Before anything explodes!

I managed to ask the woman sitting by the window—practically glued to her seat—at whose feet I had been thrown by the impact if she needed help in climbing up and out. She said she wouldn't move from her seat.

"I fought hard and long to get this window seat in Frankfurt," she said. "Under no circumstances will I give it up."

"Lady, MOVE!" I shouted. "Look outside!"

To no avail. She remained seated.

Never mind her.

But I got out of there as fast as I could manage in the tight space.

Once outside of my coach and climbing down on its undercarriage, I saw the horrendous magnitude of the accident unfold before my blurry eyes, realizing our coach's precarious position as number four on the long train, counting backward from the hissing, dying locomotive.

The reflection of the locomotive headlights still burning, bouncing off the embankment walls, and the subsequent three coaches balancing in a precarious angle gave the entire scene an eerie aspect of unforgettable dimensions.

I walked as far from this scene of horror as I could. I instinctively knew I had to get away from the disaster for fear that the large steam boiler of the stricken locomotive could blow up any second.

It didn't. The hissing of the escaping steam grew weaker. It finally ceased and, with it, the machine's headlight dimmed and ultimately died for lack of a power source.

Darkness fell over the site. I walked around in a trance, eventually huddling with other survivors close together in a corner by the embankment wall, to stay warm and seek the comfort of fellow passengers who, like me, had almost perished.

There were no rescue teams, no fire engines, no first-aid vehicles and ambulances to take away the wounded, no trucks to haul away the bodies. If they had, there would not have been enough fuel to operate them. Life in Germany then was still harsh, precarious, rationed, restricted. People in nearby Neuwied, who had been awakened by the crash, came on foot to help the wounded and comfort the dying.

I never knew how I got out of there. I experienced a severe headache. My eyes were numb, my vision blurred. I do not remember that apparently another train came to bring us survivors to Cologne, eighteen hours late. I was too much in a daze to witness and remember what went on around me.

My parents summoned their doctor at once as soon as I arrived at their house—a day late. He ordered rest. So I spent that Christmas in bed with a severe brain concussion. Gradually, my pounding headaches diminished. But I was barely with it. Christmas came and went without my fully realizing it. I spent most of the precious time with my folks lying around and resting.

Days later, my dad showed me the headlines of the Cologne newspaper of December 23: "142 people killed, over 200 injured in train accident near Neuwied," it read. "Two trains collided head-on using the same track, at speeds of sixty kilometers each."

I wasn't able to bring my dad his wine. Through the impact, the bottles in my backpack had broken.

I returned by train on January 6, 1947. Fritz came in my Opel to pick me up at the railroad station. "What happened to you? You look like cottage cheese," he burst out when he laid eyes on me.

"Yeah, and I still feel like cottage cheese too," I said before I told him the entire story.

"Boy, you live dangerously!"

EVA

❧

Shortly after returning from the fateful train ride, in February 1947, I met a young lady by the name of Eva while cross-country skiing in Germany's Black Forest. A mutual liking let us become good friends soon thereafter.

Three months later, during spring recess in early May and before I began to take summer courses at the university to prepare for my approaching graduation, she had no such schedule because she needed to augment her financial coffers to finance her next year's semesters.

Hence, Eva took a summer job as an *Au Pair*, or "house daughter" as such positions were called in the German language. It meant a mother's helper for the family, to watch the kids, wash the dishes, mop the floors and God knows what else.

The folks who chose her for the job were wealthy Swiss, living in a large, patrician home on the east side of Zürich, near the lake. The house faced a square that included a small, well kept park planted with rare bushes and flowers. (Many European cities feature such parks in residential areas. We even find them in Charleston, South Carolina, and Savannah, Georgia, bespeaking their European heritage.)

I did not take the Opel when I left Umkirch early that May to go and see her. Because there were no Army PX outlets in Switzerland and I did not have enough Swiss Francs to pay for gasoline, I hitchhiked to Zürich one Saturday morning, to be with Eva for the weekend. And this time I had no problem to cross the border, because I finally had received my American passport a month earlier

We spent Saturday afternoon and early evening together, walking through the city, watching the sun set over the lake, eating some spiced sausages on a bun with sauerkraut, washed down with a bottle of inexpensive but excellent Swiss country wine. Eventually, we found a garden restaurant where the proprietors had set up a small wooden dance floor in front of an equally small bandstand. A five-man group, consisting of brass instruments and an accordion, was going at it with a lot of humm-ta-ta, humm-ta-ta. Even some occasional yodeling.

I twirled Eva around between sips of beer until ten. The bandleader then pronounced that the place would close down for the night.

"Why?" I asked Eva.

"Because the 'Zürcher Frauenverein' sets the rules. And according to that bunch of old women, everyone should be in bed at that early bewitching hour."

"Is that actually an association of ladies of the city of Zürich?" I asked again.

"Sure is."

I brought her home at ten thirty in the evening since it was the hour of curfew imposed by the family. I waited outside until she was in her third-floor bedroom. The house was of traditional Swiss design, with living and dining rooms downstairs, as well as the kitchen and pantry; bedrooms for the family on the floor above; guest bedrooms one more flight up and the maid's quarters in the attic.

Eva occupied one of the guest bedrooms. Once up there, she opened the window to let in the mellow summer air and to lean on the windowsill to talk to me down on the street. We tried to hush our voices, so as not to disturb anyone in Eva's house, or the neighbors surrounding us. It did not last long. I heard the lady of the house calling Eva from the door of her bedroom, then saw her resolutely close her window while I quickly ducked behind some bushes. Never mind my attempts at hiding. Madame still shouted down into the plaza for me to go away, NOW!

Of course, I didn't. I had no place to go anyway. I had planned right along to stretch out on some park bench for the night. It so happened the park in front of Eva's house had one, long and nicely contoured, so I could not roll off of it in my sleep.

I was still soundly out of it the next morning when her tall, grim-faced employer rudely woke me, shaking me by my shoulder. Then he rendered a long lecture so early in the day, about such sinful things as sleeping outside in the open and the judgment of disorderly conduct and vagrancy this fact might have earned me from his neighbors around.

Well, to be truthful, I hadn't thought of that. I rubbed my eyes and said: "Good morning, Sir!" Beyond that I said nothing.

This got him even madder. He carried on, snorting like a bull in a Spanish arena being readied for the fight. When he ran out of things to say, he stared at me for a long moment. Then he snarled: "Well, I have said enough. You must be hungry. Come up and have breakfast with us. But wash your hands first."

"Yes, Sir! And thank you, Sir."

When Eva came into the dining room to bring me my boiled egg and toast, I winked an eye at her and we both barely avoided grins. But any smile would have soon disappeared anyway when our host abruptly continued his moral sermon. Breakfast had obviously given him a second wind: "Why did you not book yourself into a room at the inn? It is only two blocks away from here."

"It just did not seem that I had the time to do that, Sir. Actually, they were already closed at nine when Eva and I came back here."

I knew he did not believe me. It was too lame an excuse anyway.

"In Switzerland," he continued, as if reading my thoughts, "one either has the income to travel or one does not travel at all. Did you come by train?"

"No."

"By car then?" he continued probing.

"No, I left my car in Umkirch."

"How did you get to Zürich then?"

"Hitchhiking."

There was a long, awkward pause. It felt as if a bomb had exploded in the room. My host drilled his piercing eyes into me, deeply into my face. I responded by looking at him with the best, most sincere smile that I could muster. But I knew I had to get out of there soon. I knew I would blow my top if this continued, and that would not have done Eva any good.

Then my host finally spoke again, and he said these unforgettable words: "Do you not have any income from your capital?"

"No, Sir."

"Well, why then do you not see the necessity to sell some of your...how do you say in America for capital?...'assets,' is it, no?"

"Because I do not have any assets, Sir."

But now I had to laugh out loud, in spite of my deep frustrations with the entire course of this conversation. I couldn't keep it back anymore, which now infuriated him no end. But before he could catch his breath and go on, I swallowed my last bite of toast quickly, washed it down with the remainder of my coffee and, thanking both my hosts for breakfast, asked the lady of the house if Eva and I could be excused. She nodded gracefully.

It was Eva's off-duty day, after clearing the breakfast dishes, that is.

Our hosts had taken their Chevrolet and driven to church with their children. It was a beautiful Sunday morning. Church bells rang out all over town. People walked to the places of worship wearing their Sunday best.

When Eva finished her morning chores, we strolled down to the lake to one of several public beaches. For me, after the turmoil, violence, bombs, destruction, hunger and killing that had gone on during the last six years, to be in clean, peaceful Switzerland with a pretty woman at my side, going swimming on a Sunday morning was the fulfillment of my dreams.

The bummer came after we paid our modest entrance fees. I could fathom the need for Eva to turn right when I swung left, to reach our respective changing rooms. But as I moseyed out onto the sandy beach to look for her, I became aware of the high wooden fence running down the middle of it, dividing it into male and female sections. Now, I could understand such rules as far as changing of clothes was concerned, but found the continued segregation of the sexes rather old-fashioned and outmoded.

The dividing fence extended far out into the water, so I probed for ways to get over to the female side. "Eva, you there?" I called at the wooden blocking.

"Yeah, I am almost right across from you. This is stupid, don't you think?"

"Very stupid. Let's swim out to the end of this thing so we can do some talking."

"Okay, seems that's all we can do."

So for Eva and me to see each other and talk meant swimming far out each time and treading water while carrying on any sensible conversation. Any more intimacy was definitely out of the question.

All of Switzerland was very strict then, perhaps traditional, with moral standards set unreasonably high. Indeed it was.

Back in Freiburg, I concentrated on my summer courses during the day and helped out in Umkirch during evenings and on weekends. After Eva's return in the fall, I introduced Fritz to her while we all had some wine and pretzels at Oberkirch's on the Cathedral Plaza. Eva was visibly impressed but also taken by his presence. Fritz remembered what had happened to my relationship with Inez and stayed distant from her. He followed the same unwritten rule between friends that I had observed when I had met Inez.

But that did not stop him from joshing me about her and wanting to know all the details of our relationship, and I do mean ALL of them.

❖

Eva and I remained good friends for all these years since my journey to Zürich. She married a wealthy Porsche dealer in Lübeck , a seaport city in northern Germany. Being twenty-five years older than her, he died of cancer in the 1970s. One recent winter, she came with her significant other Eric to our home on Sanibel Island, Florida, to visit and have lunch with us. Before I grilled burgers on the patio, we sipped Bloody Marys while lounging in our deck chairs on a day in January when the temperature stood at 82 degrees.

Hanna was at first cool to the idea but quickly warmed up as it became evident that Eva and I were just that—old friends. After lunch when we walked the short distance to the beach, many a male head in my neighborhood turned to take another look at her elegant stride and gracious face, older now but still beautiful.

After a long battle with leukemia, she bade her final farewell to us on March 7, 1999.

THE ROYAL WEDDING

❧

In late May of 1947, shortly after my return from the Zürich weekend and after finishing our spring semester, Fritz said: "I am invited to a wedding."

"Oh? Where?"

"At my cousin's, the Princess von Thurn und Taxis."

"Aren't they over near Regensburg?"

"Yes. We could drive there on Friday, stop in Sigmaringen to stay at Josefslust Mansion with my parents, then drive on Saturday. It's only half a day's drive from there. The roads are clear. I inquired. You want to come along?"

"Why not at the Hohenzollern Burg?"

"We can't. The French Army is in there. They confiscated the Burg immediately after the war ended. You remember when the government of General Petain still occupied the castle? They shipped him back to France and installed their army headquarters there."

"But I'm not invited to the wedding," I said.

"Yes, you are. I took care of that."

"I don't have anything appropriate to wear."

"Neither do I. It doesn't matter. We'll get it at their place."

"Okay. Let's bring it on."

That Saturday during mid-afternoon, I maneuvered the old Opel across a narrow bridge into the inner courtyard of the Thurn and Taxis residency. It was an old castle, centuries old. Like my mother's family mansion, Landfort in Holland, it was built in the fourteenth century and used to be a water burg, surrounded by a deep moat and equipped with turret-like towers on all four corners. It was designed that way to see the enemy approach, then fight him without being seen.

When I crossed the bridge, I could detect out of the corner of my eye that the moat was still filled with water. But as at Landfort, the turret towers were gone. The building had been modernized and expanded.

As soon as I had navigated the inner courtyard's circle to the front entrance, two male servants appeared from nowhere. One tried to open the door on Fritz's side. But I knew that door stuck and needed a special lifting up a notch to open. Before the servant caught on, Fritz had done it from the inside.

The valet on my side managed to open my door but it immediately sagged down a couple of inches. It was so old, tired and worn out!

Fritz's servant asked for our luggage.

"We don't have any," said Fritz to the valet, "just the small duffel on the back seat."

"For both of you?"

"Yes. No problem. We'll sleep in the same room. So please take it up to where we sleep."

"But Your Highness, you will sleep in another room than your friend."

"Oh, I didn't expect that. We can share a room. We always do."

"That is fine for you. But Her Highness, the *Fürstin*, has decided otherwise."

"It's okay, Fritz," I said, "I'll take my toothbrush and comb out of the bag."

"You will not have to do that, sir," the servant on my side said, "because all of that will be available at your room."

I turned around to face him. "What's your name?"

"Call me Johann, or Hans if you want."

"How about my car? Where do I park it?" I asked him, still avoiding to call him by name. Hans seemed too informal. I'd probably settle on Johann.

"The head chauffeur will take it to the garage."

This, I realized, was going to be an interesting visit!

Our servants guided us to our rooms. It was three-ten in the afternoon. My valet waited behind me to grab my old Loden coat. It hadn't been cleaned in years and showed the effects of many bloody hunting trips. He hung it in a spacious closet. Then he turned down the bed, drew the curtains so that the room was almost pitch-dark, bowed and said: "I wish you a good rest. I will come back at 17:00 to assist you in dressing for the evening."

ME? Sleep? Now? Dress? I didn't have anything to wear except what I already had on. This was becoming more interesting by the minute.

I opened the curtains again and read a book. At four, I really got sleepy so I lay down and dropped off at once. From deep dreams I awoke when I heard someone tiptoe through my room into my private bath. Then the water began to rush into the tub. It had to be my valet. What in hell is he doing? I wondered.

Then he tiptoed back to my bedside and almost whispered: "Sir, it is time to awake and take a bath. I have filled the tub for you. Lavender and other soaps of various scents are laid out on a table next to the tub. I will return in half an hour to assist you with dressing."

TO ASSIST ME WITH DRESSING? It couldn't be true.

I heard him come back when I was still lounging in my hot bathtub. As I reentered my bedroom wrapped in a super-sized bath towel, he stood erect near the door, head bowed.

"Everything you need is laid out here on your bed. It should fit. I will wait here to assist you."

"You don't have to do that, Johann. Johann? Isn't that your name?"

"Yes, Sir."

I looked at my king-size bed. There it was: a complete tuxedo, cummerbund, suspenders, black bow tie, starched white shirt with a rippled chest inlay, skivvies, black socks, highly polished black shoes.

"Where did all this come from?"

"From our central *Gardrobe* storage room."

"The pants probably don't fit. I have wide shoulders and a narrow waist, so I need a large jacket and 32-inch waist pants."

"It is all there. While you slept, I measured your clothes and received the right sizes from our supply. But if anything doesn't fit correctly, I'll go back and bring the right size."

I finally caved in: "Well, if that is so, Johann, you better stick around and help me get into this uniform."

At once Johann opened the stiffly starched white shirt and held it high for me to slip my hands through its sleeves. He grinned happily to have won me over.

At ten minutes to six, Johann finished dressing me, then pointed to the full-sized mirror inside the bathroom door. "Please, Sir, take a look. And tell me if everything is satisfactory to you."

I stared at myself in the mirror and still remember my silent, unexpected surge of delight at how I looked. This was the first time I had ever worn a tuxedo. Many times I had seen my dad in one when he and Mom went out to formal dinners. But that was when I was growing up. Then the war came and such things as wearing formal dress were forgotten. Now I had my first time at it.

The tuxedo fit to a T. I looked more slender than I really was. And I certainly was not obese, had good muscle tone, wide shoulders and a narrow waist. The deep, freckled tan on my entire six-foot frame, generated from many summer months of outside tractor work in the fields when I did not wear a shirt, now emerged on my face, neck and hands in a stunning contrast to the snow-white dress shirt Johann had helped me into. I even had my unruly, wavy, short-cropped red hair brushed down hard with the help of lots of Vitalis, or whatever Johann had on the shelf for that purpose. Too bad Eva couldn't see me now. She would have loved it.

A bit of male vanity? Sure, we are all human!

"Yes, Johann, you made me look *herrlich, wunderbar*. My *Tischdame* tonight will love it. Do you know who she is?"

Johann was silent for a while, and visibly embarrassed. He tried to be so grown up but was still so young: twenty or twenty-one, maybe. His humble upbringing did not include conversing with members of high society. And as a guest of his famous employers but nevertheless a commoner, in his world, I was just that. He was taught to serve, not converse. Yet, mindful of the teachings of my stern but loving mother, I considered everyone, including Johann, my equal, my peer. His German was heavily accented Bavarian. With me he tried to speak the high German as he was instructed to do, even though his tongue was struggling with it. But when he became excited, he'd fall back into more Bavarian-oriented language, as he did now when he finally answered my question: "A very pretty young lady, Sir."

"So everything is okay, very okay?" I laughed at him.

"Ja, okay, ich weiss," he said with shiny eyes. He produced an ever-so-faint smile of satisfaction about my praising him. Obviously, he was not used to a guest paying him a compliment.

At five minutes to six, Johann guided me downstairs to a set of double doors, where other servants stood ready to open the gate to paradise.

"I will be waiting out here for you at 22:00, when the banquet will be over, to assist you for your night's rest."

Such precision! I didn't fight it anymore. I knew I would lose. By now I really liked the man. So I just smiled at him and said: "That will be fine. Thank you, Johann."

It was an elegant affair. One hundred guests were assembled in the large reception hall of the castle where Moet Champagne was served in tall, narrow glasses along with small tidbits of hors d'oeuvres of mostly Russian Caviar. I looked for my buddy Fritz. I was the only commoner in the room. I needed his reassurance because I felt somewhat forlorn in this sea of royalty. But he had already spotted me and made his way to me through the crowd. He looked totally elegant, even a bit royal, in his tuxedo. I had never seen him in one. He grinned and burst out: "Man, oh man, did they dress you too? But hey, you look spiffy. I've never seen you look like that."

"So do you. Did you rest well when the servant put you to bed to lullaby?" I grinned.

"Hell no. I climbed out of my window and down the wooden lattice where the ivy grows up the wall. Then I moseyed over to the garage. I knew where it was from my last visit a few years back. You know, they have one that has room for ten cars. They have some beauties in there. I'll show you tomorrow when we have more time," explained Fritz.

"Did you get back in time?"

"Sure did. My valet never knew I was gone," he said.

"Too bad you didn't come over to take me along."

Just then, a stately older couple, followed by the bride and groom, walked over to us and greeted Fritz, expressing their joy in seeing him. Then my pal turned around to me at his side and said: "Here, let me introduce you to my uncle and aunt, the *Fürst* and *Fürstin* von *Thurn und Taxis,* and the bride, of course, and her man of choice. The *Fürstin* is my aunt because she is my mother's sister."

Ah, so. She was another daughter of the last King Albert of Saxony. Like Fritz's mother, she was a Prinzessin von Sachsen before she married.

The *Fürstin* stretched out her hand in a slightly upward motion with its back facing me, a sure sign she expected me to kiss her hand. I remembered my manners from my mom's teachings, stood very erect then slightly bent my head, held her hand loosely and ever so lightly touched my lips on her soft, lavender-soaped skin.

But I never clicked my heels as would have been the proper behavior according to centuries-old German militaristic tradition. That show of respect was just a bit too much for me to swallow.

"Highness, *Durchlaucht*, I am very pleased to meet you. And I wish to express my sincerest thanks for inviting me to witness this marvelous event," I stammered, a bit in awe over all these important people talking to a simple commoner like me. "And of course, hello to you as well," I added for the young couple who were about my age.

Thirty minutes later, when the servants opened the two-winged doors to the large dining room, they called out: *"Messieurs et Mesdames, le diner est servie."*

A narrow table was set up to the right of the entrance displaying fifty small cards showing the names of the gentlemen's escorts for the evening. My card listed a young lady with no aristocratic designation except the "von" between her first and last name, the lowest rank in German aristocracy.

I looked for my *Tischdame*. Her first name was Sigrid and she turned out to be young, pretty and vivacious. I held out my right arm and she slid hers through mine and squeezed twice, a silent signal I knew: although I had fire-engine red hair and lots of freckles, she thought I was cute. I had no problem with that small and silent dialogue. I walked her to our assigned seats.

Not far away from the center, I helped Sigrid seat herself then sat down on my chair, which was held by another servant. But my position so far away from the table's edge seemed uncomfortable so I pulled the chair closer. Immediately thereafter, I felt a tapping on my shoulder and heard a servant whisper into my ear: "Sir, would you mind to get up for a second so I can arrange your chair?"

I did and noticed he pulled it back to where he had set it in the first place. And that was where markers on the ancient, huge Persian rug showed him the chair's position. Puzzled, I checked both sides and witnessed that ALL chairs were at the same distance from the edge of the table, lined up like members of Germany's Elite Cavalry at a royal parade.

Thus were the strictest of all adherences to centuries-old traditions.

The table was set for one hundred guests, the *Fürst* on one end, the *Fürstin* on the other. The bride and groom sat at the table's center facing each other. Fritz, as the highest-ranking guest, had the pleasure of guiding the bride to the table, then sat on her left. I could clearly see him diagonally across the long table. He looked bored. I knew that look. So when he turned his head towards me again, I raised my thumb. I knew that would cheer him up. He just shrugged, laughed, raised his eyebrows and looked at the bride. I knew that too. He was wishing he had a *Tischdame* like mine next to him and not the bride of someone else.

Over more caviar and toast and similar other tidbits available nowhere else in Germany at that time, Sigrid pointed to my name card in front of my plate near the five various wine and champagne glasses and a sizable array of silverware: "Fritz told me that your name is Gerd. But now I see your name card lists you as GERHARD PETER CASPAR HILGER – VON AMERIKA. Why Gerd then?"

"Gerd is the abbreviation of Gerhard. And I am called by that name only in Germany."

"So I can call you Gerd, too. How about Peter?"

"Peter appears in every generation of our family since 1594," I replied, thinking it would make me a touch more respectable in this name-calling, lineage-oriented society. "In those long-ago days, my last name was Heiliger."

"Saint. But you don't look saintly to me," she smiled with a tantalizing throw-back of her head. "But the Caspar is spelled wrong here as well. It should be Kasper."

"You remember the German spelling of that name. Mine is spelled the English way. It occurred in every generation of my family since 1720. Our last name was then Hilliger. The English American version is the way it is written on my card."

"So how did that happen?"

"Because my father was born in the United States. He is American. I was born in Düsseldorf but am American as well."

"Heavens. I never met an American. But you are charming. I thought all Americans were 'different.'"

Hearing that statement, I was inclined to ask her how Americans are "different" but did not pursue the subject any further. Instead I switched our conversation to easier matters, like where she lived, where she stayed here in Regensburg, whether she had a steady boyfriend, things guys are interested in when they meet pretty girls.

After a seven-course dinner and over coffee and cognac, servants came around with silver boxes holding Cuban cigars and American Camel cigarettes, both a rarity in postwar Germany. I watched Fritz not take one, but a whole handful of the latter to put one between his lips and the others in his pocket. So I knew we would have something to smoke tomorrow when we returned.

At exactly 2200 hours, the *Fürstin* rose, nodded to the assembled guests and sailed to the door with her long emerald green chiffon gown trailing her footsteps on the Persian rug. Her husband followed close behind.

"That was it," Fritz grinned. "Let's go upstairs. I snatched a bottle of wine and hid it from the eyes of my valet in my bathroom."

"It's a deal."

I let Johann take me to my room, where the towels had been changed to fresh ones and the bedding had been turned down. Climbing up the stairs, I asked him: "Johann, tell me. How did you know I am from America?"

"The head chauffeur told us. He saw your American emblems on the front and rear of your car."

"Then I must presume they also found out my name?"

"Yes, they read it from your car registration, which apparently is wrapped around your car's steering wheel post."

So the networking among the staff had been activated again.

"Smart," I said, although I was not altogether happy about this unexpected intelligence work.

When things quieted down on the second floor, I opened my door again, made sure everybody was asleep and snuck over two doors to Fritz's quarters.

He got the wine out of the bathroom, but as we settled down, we noticed another bottle and one glass had been set on a silver tray at a table near his bed.

"I guess we've got enough to drink," he said. We lifted our glasses and toasted ourselves: "Here is to us, *Plisch und Plum!*"

That was what Fritz's mother the *Fürstin* often called us. Wilhelm Busch, 1832 – 1908, invented these names. Around the second half of the 19th century, he was a well-known German writer of children's books, most of them stories told in drawings. *Plisch und Plum* were two of the characters he used, two little dogs that were always getting into trouble. As far as I can tell, he wrote about them in 1884.

"Yeah. Here is to us," I concluded, clinking glasses with my buddy.

The wedding ceremony took place the next morning, a Sunday, immediately following the ten o'clock mass in the majestic Cathedral Dom of Regensburg. We drove to church with the Opel cleanly washed and sparkling, something that hadn't happened in years.

Plisch and Plum were separated, as I expected and found okay. As the highest-ranking guest, he was seated in the first pew next to the *Fürstin von Thurn und Taxis*, the mother of the bride. I was shown to a seat in the twelfth pew among other guests I had met the night before.

But then I spotted Sigrid not far away and moved over to her, sat next to her close and snuggled up. Everyone smiled and made room for me, because romance was the message of the day, and oldsters always like young romances.

Fritz and I left immediately after the service and drove home the way we came.

RETURN TO FREIBURG

⚜

In June of 1947, following my return from Regensburg, my trusted Opel gave out. It just expired! Nobody had parts for it anymore. I didn't even know how many miles it had run. I sold it for 6,000 marks, a currency in a wild spin of inflation, by that time equal to eight pounds of butter or eight packs of Lucky Strike.

I stayed with Fritz in Umkirch that entire summer. We considered it a summer vacation without work, without having to get up early, without commitments. We hunted what was there to hunt. We raised litters of more puppies born to our German shorthair pointers. We swam, read, played with rehabbing Ante-WW II-model cars retrieved from junkyards.

In short, we relaxed as we had never before allowed ourselves to do. At that time, Max and I were the only ones left, as was brother Franz, of course, since Umkirch was his home as well. Everyone else had moved back to their families or to other towns and universities.

But with the start of the fall semester in October 1947, now without wheels, I too moved out of Umkirch and back to Freiburg, where I took a room in a boarding house near campus. I used the train then to get to and fro, or my bike for shorter distances. I wouldn't have another car until

I arrived in Washington, DC in September 1950.

On June 21, 1948, Germany woke up to a new currency. It was a well-kept secret that only a very few government people and bankers knew. Because of increasing tensions between West and East, a uniform German reform of her currency became impossible to achieve. Therefore, the measure, led by Washington, was conceived and developed by the western Allies for their occupation zones only.

The financial action was called a *Waehrungsreform*—"currency reform." With the official exchange rate pegged at RM 4.20 per dollar, the old, tired RM (Reichsmark) had reached a level of over 10,000 RM to a dollar in free trading. That set the inflation rate at 1,160%.

Yet, as related earlier, my tuition per semester up to that time had amounted to the nominal amount of a mere RM 200.00, in my barter-trade currency equal to half a pound of butter or ten Lucky Strike cigarettes. The system badly needed an overhaul, a reform as a result of economic actions that began with Hitler's endless printing of new monies without the corresponding coverage of gold, then continued into the war years and ended in an almost total financial undermining of the German industrial potential at war's end in 1945.

That day in 1948, Germans were directed over the radio to go to prearranged locations in their towns and villages to receive the new currency. For handing over RM 400.00, each individual would receive as pocket money 40.00 *Deutsche Mark* as the new bills and coins were named. An additional maximum of 2,000 Reichsmark could be exchanged into the Deutschmark a month later. After that, all cash in Reichsmark became worthless.

Obligations, Bonds and Treasury notes were fixed at ten percent of their old value. Real Estate went through the reform on a 1:1 basis, i.e. it was worth before the reform the same as it was thereafter—if a buyer could be found who had that much money in *Deutschmark*. Other real monies as stocks or land were left to find their new values in a money market now freed of most government restrictions. So was the exchange rate between the Dollar and the *Deutschmark*.

Fortunes were lost that day, but new fortunes grew out of the measure. Germany entered the era of free markets. The new currency Deutsche Mark swiftly established itself as solid and non-inflationary and later became one of the hardest in the world. We called it the Deutschmark.

And with it, my financial situation changed drastically as well: the Black Market became a thing of the past! I returned to the status of a dirt-poor student!

The Russians, miffed at the actions of their western Allies, introduced a reform of the *Reichsmark* in their eastern occupation zone three days later. It was called *Deutsche Mark der Deutschen Notenbank*—translated in English as "German Mark of the German National Bank." Simultaneously, on the same day, June 24, 1948, they closed all land and waterway accesses to Berlin, in violation of the Potsdam Agreement. Their aim was the total control of the old German capital. The Berlin Blockade had started.

The following day, June 25, under the command of General Lucius D. Clay, the first American Douglas DC-4 cargo plane flew to the encircled city with supplies. In all, 277,728 flights by the U.S. and British Air Forces brought in 2.1 million tons of anything the citizens of Berlin needed, including those large shipments of corn, the result of that earlier misunderstanding. The Russians conceded on May 4, 1949, at the United Nations in New York and lifted the blockade, but imposed even narrower air corridors into Berlin's Tempelhof Airport, which they cautioned the western Allies to strictly observe.

❖

In 1990, East and West Germany were re-united to form the Republic of Germany. Berlin became the new capital. The eastern Deutsche Mark was exchanged into Deutschmark at the ratio of three for one.

In 2002, the Deutschmark was merged into the new European currency, the Euro, and thus ceased to exist.

❖

In late October of 1948, I was supposed to prepare for my MBA written and oral exams. They were scheduled for November and December respectively, with graduation planned in time for Christmas. I was nearing the end of many years of learning and eager to get it over with.

But one day in early December—written exams already behind me and orals still to do—a young lady I knew, from Neufchatel, Switzerland, walked into my room at the boarding house where I lived. I had met her briefly before through a mutual friend. Her name was Antoinette. She was determined to spend as much of her father's money as humanly possible. Her father, I was sure, was hard at work to keep up with her spending habits while manufacturing Swiss wrist and other watches.

She was also quite attractive, a fact which helped.

But what impressed me most about her to that point was a beautiful, shiny, snow-white Mercedes Benz convertible with red leather seats. She swept me off my feet by persuading me to come along on a little fall trip through the Alps in her sporty roadster. I willingly succumbed.

In Switzerland, which has plenty of Alps, she couldn't travel with a male friend. Such un-heard-of things were done in France. Switzerland then was even more moral than now. Sort of dull, I thought. I remembered it from my weekend with Eva in Zürich the year before.

I didn't have a dime to spare. She did, though, plenty of them. We took many detours to reach Salzburg, Austria, our easternmost destination. We checked in for three days at the Grand Hotel. It lay opposite the Mirabelle Palace, where the Dukes of Hapsburg entertained their lady friends while their wives and families stayed in the confines of their grey fortress on the mountaintop above town.

And we went to hear the Vienna Philharmonic Orchestra at the *Festspielhaus* every night, to witness Maestro Karl Boehm conduct Mozart. All Mozart, of course. Mozart is everywhere in Salzburg.

It was Heaven on Earth!

I was exhausted when I returned. And my loving mother scolded me good and hard when I got back, because she had phoned my boarding house on numerous occasions and never found me home.

AUF WIEDERSEHEN, GERMANY
BON JOUR, PARIS

⌘

I n late December of 1948, I graduated with a degree in Economics and Law. I never did get good marks during either exam. But I did pass, in spite of my state of complete exhaustion.

Christmas break gave me relief and a chance to sleep before going to Paris, where I had received—through my economics Professor Eucken's recommendation—a scholarship from La Sorbonne's Ecole du Droit, for postgraduate work in *Science Politique and Droit*, political sciences and law, at its prestigious Law School on Boulevard St. Michel.

The same year, Fritz was invited to study at the University of Geneva in Switzerland. He stayed there until the spring of 1950. He married a great-grand niece of the last Czar of Russia immediately thereafter.

Great friendships had been made. Fritz and I had enjoyed a wonderful time, first rough then peaceful, in Umkirch and Freiburg. But now, finally, it was time to go, to move on.

I could hardly wait!

On New Year's Day of 1949, I departed by train for Paris, eager to leave Germany behind for good—the country and all that had happened there.

More than a year and a half later, after completing school with a master's degree in law, I boarded the *S/S Argentina* in Cherbourg on September 2, 1950, and left Europe for Washington, DC, then on to Chicago, Illinois.

An era in my life had come to a close. But I knew that those friendships, forged in the heat of war and its aftermath, would last way beyond my departure.

And indeed they did!

THE END

EPILOGUE

❧

After a long bout with cancer, Max von Waldburg zu Wolfegg died in 1988, his magnificent Hercules physique reduced to just skin and bones.

Franz von Hohenzollern expired of old age in 1989.

Georg von Mecklenburg succumbed to heart failure in 1991.

Konstantin von Bayern died when he crashed his private plane upon landing at Munich's Riem Airport in 1995.

Gero von Sachsen died of cancer in 1999.

Timo von Sachsen suffered a fatal heart attack in 2002.

Albert Joshua Burger visited Fritz in 2000 and proclaimed he would stay with him for a month or two. As in 1945 when we had no choices, it didn't work. Fritz tired of him in two days and asked him to leave. He has not been heard from since.

Both Fritz and I lost contact with Kurt.

But my old friend Fritz's health declined. It was increasing blindness that bothered him the most. He needed large TV screens to read my letters. When I began to write this book, I often sent him excerpts to read. And always he remembered more details and additional stories of our mutual lives that I had forgotten.

Then at Christmas 2009, his greetings were printed out and he just signed his name—barely. Then his letters ceased coming.

In his residence, Josefslust outside Sigmaringen, he went to sleep on September 16, 2010, and never woke up again. My soulmate had died.

My friend of sixty-seven years was gone. The Fürst von Hohenzollern was gone. The new Fürst von Hohenzollern was now Karl Friederich, his oldest son.

Long before all these events, I had written a letter to his longtime secretary Frau Koch. She was French but had married a German. I always spoke French to her. So I even wrote her in French that she should notify me when Fritz's health indicated the end of his life. I wanted to be there for him before or surely after his passing—to be with him in my thoughts.

Frau Koch called me the day before he died. She called Sanibel. My voice mail was off. She called Hendersonville. My voice mail was off. It's always off when I am not home. I was on a trip to Iowa and Minnesota at the time. I came home on the day of his funeral, September 26. Too late to fly to Sigmaringen, where 780 people gathered in the Erlöser Hedingen Cathedral to attend the High Mass Requiem.

In church, his three sons had kept the seat next to Ferdinand, the youngest, reserved for me. I could not get there in time. The seat remained empty.

Fritz's coffin was escorted down to the church's Gruft, the crypt where all his ancestors for the last 800 years were resting.

So now, as I complete this saga in October 2010, we Umkirch "Buddies" from the war are down to just one.

Me.

www.ingramcontent.com/pod-product-compliance
Lightning Source LLC
LaVergne TN
LVHW011228080426
835509LV00005B/377